Georgina 'Georgie' Peterson was born and raised in Liverpool, U.K. She has a Bachelor of Arts degree in English and also has a strong background in performing arts and working with children, both of which have greatly influenced her life and career. In her late-teens, Georgie was diagnosed with a rare brain disorder. Although she continues to face many obstacles, Georgie considers herself lucky – to be creative, to be alive and to be surrounded by such great people.

She is currently penning another book, which she hopes will become her debut novel, and continues to work on raising awareness of illness and disability, mental health, bullying and so on.

Follow Georgie on Instagram @georgiepeterson and Twitter @G_Peterson1

You can also check out her website: www.georgiepeterson.com

Thank you.

Dedication

For everybody I love, without whom, I wouldn't have the courage to share my story.

Georgina Peterson

FREAKS LIKE ME

AUSTIN MACAULEY PUBLISHERS™

LONDON • CAMBRIDGE • NEW YORK • SHARJAH

A CIP catalogue record for this title is available from the British Library.

ISBN 9781788785952 (Paperback)
ISBN 9781788785969 (Hardback)
ISBN 9781788785976 (E-Book)

www.austinmacauley.com

First Published (2018)
Austin Macauley Publishers Ltd™
25 Canada Square
Canary Wharf
London
E14 5LQ

Acknowledgements

Firstly, I want to thank all of you for reading my book. Becoming a published writer was beyond my wildest dreams. While I am so grateful to see my words in print, *Freaks Like Me* always felt like a huge risk. But in the end, it is a risk I am willing to take, because I believe in it. I believe in the message I am trying to send out into the world, and I hope, with all of my heart, that my words have helped you.

Thank you to everyone at Austin Macauley for taking a chance on a first-time, unknown author. Thank you for answering all of my anxious questions and, most of all, thank you for the happiness I feel as I am writing these words.

To my incredible doctors, thank you for your constant support and reassurance. To all of the mental health specialists I have been a patient of, I'm sorry I couldn't talk about all of you, but I thank you equally for helping me to see the world in a brighter light.

To all of the emergency call handlers, fast response teams, paramedics, nurses, nurse assistants, doctors, radiologists, phlebotomists, plaster cast technicians and hospital volunteers, thank you for everything you have done for me and for so many others. (Also, I'm really sorry I got hysterical that time and pulled my neck brace off!)

A massive thank you to my lovelies, old and new. I love and value each and every one of our friendships. To LN, because when I was alone, you came into my life and lit up my saddened soul. Also, thank you for introducing me to some of the awesome people I now call friends too. To HG, for your constant understanding and for reading and replying to all of my long, complicated messages. To LW, because you knew me before it happened, and you stayed. To PH, TW, SW and LH, for accepting me exactly as I am. Thank you for taking me (and my family!) into your beautiful circle.

To my hair stylist, thank you for washing and braiding my hair every few days when I injured both of my arms, and for scrubbing that medical superglue out of my scalp. To my beautician, thank you for all of our treatment room chats, for not waxing my eyebrows off when I had seizures in there, and of course, thank you for making me feel pretty. You are both great friends to me, and at this point, you both deserve certificates in dealing with seizures!

To those I don't see regularly but who never fail to check up on me, thank you. You know who you are, and it truly means the world to me.

To my wonderful family – by this point, you will have received personalised notes of pure gratitude, so here, I'll keep it short: thank you for always being the ones who lift me up every time I fall (literally *and* figuratively). It's all for you guys!

But I must give an extra special mention to my mum: thank you for always believing in me, especially when I couldn't believe in myself. You could always see the light, and that means everything.

Last, but by no means least, to Erin, who would have loved this, and to my granddad, who would have been so proud, thank you both for showing me what brave really is.

All my love,
G
Xox

Prologue

"I can't split myself into a million pieces! Don't you get that? I can't please everyone!"

With that, I'm quiet, and I put my head down. I've upset her, and that's the last thing I wanted to do. There is silence in my mind. Just for a moment.

"Wow...we've hit a new level of pathetic just now! You're so stupid and selfish. You'll never learn, will you?" I knew the voice would return. It always does.

I run upstairs to my bedroom, to escape from the situation, but really, I'm trying to hide from the unrecognisable person I've become.

My back leans against the wall and then, my body falls until I'm seated on the floor. I'm shaking. My head is spinning and my heart is thumping faster and heavier...

I know it's coming, but I don't know at the same time. It's difficult to explain, because at some point, unknown to me, my mind just blanks out.

"Stop it! Stop pulling at your hands right now!" somebody yells. They hold my hands together in a grip they have made with their own.

Slowly, I am returning.

I know what happened before, because the feelings are still there. Anxiety still rushes through my veins as I try to catch my breath.

"That's it, in and out," they say, showing me how to breathe, showing me how to come back.

"I don't know what I did," I say to my mum, crying now, "or what I said."

She strokes the baby hairs back from my red, sweaty face and says, "I'll tell you later."

Afterwards, I lie on my bed in the quiet of my bedroom, waiting for 'later' to arrive, fearing all of the possibilities. How can I just lose time like that? How can I not know what I've said, or done, or what other people have said to me?

"Because you're pathetic," the voice tells me, not that I need to be reminded, and I cry again.

That was one of my many panic attacks, each as destructive as the one before.

Usually, it didn't take much to set me off. This was just something my sister said. Basically, I wanted us to spend more time together. I felt like she was becoming more distant from me with every passing day, but because she was so busy and felt like everybody wanted something from her, she snapped. She's only human.

My sister wasn't mean to me, but I was hypersensitive. Everything that *could* have been taken as a negative opinion of me, or a criticism, a rejection or a disagreement, and I'd just break.

It could have been a very obvious joke, and sometimes, it didn't even have to be words: it could have been a funny look, real or imagined, but I'd feel devastated and disliked, fearing what other people could see when they looked at me.

Could they see the damage? Could they see the pain behind my eyes?

But I knew the answer – *no*. And it was 'no' because I'd developed a really good system of pretence. I wasn't the image of depression or anxiety. In public, I didn't fit any stigma of mental illness.

But in private, I wanted to die…

Part One
Before

Chapter One

One thing that is for certain about me? I was intentional. I *am* intentional.

My mother had a miscarriage before me, and it devastated her. She wanted another baby, so she was ecstatic when she found out she was pregnant again. Eight months, thirteen days, eleven hours and forty-five minutes later, I was here. I *am* here, and I like to think I'm here for a reason.

I love the fact that I was planned and purposefully brought into the world, and born into a family I love with all of my heart. I was named after my great-grandmother, a formidable matriarch, and she had thirteen children. Thirteen! Between them, my nan and granddad had seventeen siblings, fifteen of whom were girls. So, as I'm sure you can imagine, my family is gigantic. The stories I've heard about the generations of Peterson's that came before me are legendary, not always for the right reasons, but legendary all the same.

We are a pretty happy, supportive family, but of course, there are some broken connections, a few issues that may never be resolved, and everybody ends up closer to some than they are to others. But we all love each other. We're all there, and whilst we have found our own ways in life, and followed our own paths, our family – the importance of family – is the foundation.

My mum's pregnancy was plain-sailing (her words, not mine!), but from the moment she held me, she was scared that something was going to happen to me. She has never been able to explain it; she just says she felt an overwhelming sense of fear. I was a clingy baby, and I don't know if that was an accidental effect of her fear, or if it's just the way I was. I was very affectionate too. They say I've 'always loved a good hug!'

I am a summer baby and I always feel much happier when the sun comes out. We even used to joke that I had a terrible case of S.A.D (seasonal affective disorder) because when the weather was horrid, I genuinely did feel sad. Considering I live in England, with its accurate rainy reputation, I'm sure I'd always be feeling down and dreary if I really did suffer with S.A.D. My nursery nurse used to call me 'Miss Sunshine' because I was always smiling once I'd settled in. She said I reminded her of the sunshine baby from the *Teletubbies*!

Something else that made me happy was stories. I was obsessed and always wanted multiple bedtime stories. As far back as my family can remember, I nearly always had a book in my hand. As a little toddler, I already knew the alphabet inside out, both ways. The nursery nurses were pretty impressed with that!

Chapter Two

As a young woman, my mum was a residential social worker. She worked with disabled children, neglected children and underprivileged children, and it was everything she'd ever wanted from her career. She continued for a while after she'd had her first daughter, my sister Ellie, but for a few days every week, she had to leave her baby with our grandparents, and in the end, she decided to move back home permanently, settling for a standard 9 to 5 nearby.

I know I'm biased, but she is one of the most incredible women I have ever known. She has the biggest, kindest heart, and even in the most difficult situations, she never once wavered from being a great mum. My goals and aspirations have changed many times, but one dream has always remained the same: I want to be a mother. That's not because I feel some kind of pressure, or because there is an age-old expectation of motherhood due to the fact that I was born female. It's because I have spent my entire life watching this woman standing on her own two feet, working tirelessly, raising her children and being brilliant at it.

So someday, when I'm ready, I know I'll have the best role model to show me the way.

As a child, my sister was a bit of a spoilt brat. Ellie had always been the centre of attention, never having to share the spotlight, and she loved it that way. I think it's safe to say she wasn't exactly thrilled when I came along and crashed that party. (Of course, it worked out pretty well for me!) Ellie would have her friends over and they would pretend they were the Spice Girls, singing into their hairbrushes and dancing around like they were starring in music videos. I always got to be Baby Spice. I love my memories with 'the big girls'. I really admired one of her lifelong best friends. She was crazy, outgoing and awesome, and I wanted to be like her when I grew up. But deep down, I never looked up to anybody more than I looked up to my big sister.

I just loved being with her, even though it drove Ellie crazy sometimes. I'd find out which boys she fancied and tease her about it, and I'd 'borrow' her lipsticks and gel pens and CDs, but she pushed me down the stairs on a space hopper once, so I think we're even! Ellie will forever argue that I fell, or that my fear signals hadn't fully developed yet. There is an endless debate about it, but I'm convinced: she definitely pushed me!

A few years later, I got to be a big sister too. Our mum gave birth to another daughter, another sister, and I have suffered from 'middle child syndrome' ever since. When my mum told me that she had a baby growing inside her tummy, or however pregnancy is explained to a five-year-old, I decided that I really wanted a baby brother. But when Mia came along, I soon got over it. She was just too cute with her honey-coloured curls and her deep-brown eyes.

As I got older and had my own friends around, I realised that Ellie had a point: having a younger sister can definitely be annoying sometimes! Think about it – you're an anxious kid anyway, trying to be cool with your friends, but your little sister just keeps showing up, acting weird, demanding their attention, and it didn't help that they actually liked her! My friends would say she was adorable and I'd smile, secretly contemplating all the things that made her the total opposite. Mia wanted to be part of everything I did when I had my friends over, even though she barely had the time of day for me when I was on my own!

Sundays – the only day that none of us were busy – were reserved for roast dinners at our grandparents' house. Mia and I would put on little shows for our family after lunch. That was always fun, and I loved being able to boss her around for a few hours with no consequences.

When we moved house, Mia and I had to share a bedroom. I wasn't thrilled, not at all, especially because Ellie got to swan around in a bedroom that was all her own. The worst thing about sharing a room with Mia was the snoring. Oh, the snoring... I knew it wasn't her fault of course, but I don't think I had a full night's sleep for years!

Sharing also meant I had to compromise on decoration. I certainly wasn't into *The Tweenies* or *Clifford The Big Red Dog*, both of which would soon be part of our bedroom. "But mum, she changes her mind all the time!" I'd complain, adamant that it wasn't fair. I'd planned it to be decorated in homage to Gryffindor, but I just ended up with some *Harry Potter* wall stickers. I used to imagine a wall being built right in the centre of our room. Mia could be in her obnoxiously bright bedroom, talking to her beloved Clifford, and I could quietly immerse myself in the world that J.K. Rowling invented for us.

Our room was the opposite of peaceful. As much as my mum tried to keep it decluttered, there was never enough space to accommodate everything. I have always been very sentimental, so I wanted to keep every single thing (cinema tickets, doodles, stickers, good behaviour badges, photographs, favourite clothes that I'd outgrown a long time ago, favourite fluffy pens that had run out of ink etc.), and I wanted it all in my bedroom.

On top of that, Mia was the type of kid who accidentally messed the room up ten seconds after it had been tidied. She was quite rebellious to my goodie-two-shoes personality. One of my favourite bedtime books was a collection of short stories titled *My Naughty Little Sister,* and it really could have been based on us!

Mia was somehow born with the rare ability to be oblivious to what anybody else thinks. Even as a teenager, she couldn't have cared less. She did her own thing, and she never concerned herself with what other people might say about her. I always admired that. She was, and remains to be, fiercely protective too. As for Ellie, I looked up to her in so many ways – for example, she was always so self-assured. As we grew up, I learnt that she did have insecurities of her own, of course, but she just exuded this humble confidence, and I wished I'd have that someday.

Despite their annoying ways, I know I struck lucky with my sisters. I really can't imagine my life – past, present and future – without them by my side.

Chapter Three

Our dad, Peter, wasn't a particularly active parent. They married when Mia was a toddler, and I remember waking up that morning, excitement rising within us all. Mia and I wore matching bridesmaid dresses with little embroidered flowers, matching sandals too, and Ellie wore a more grown-up outfit. I was allowed to invite a few of my friends to the wedding party, and we had a lot of fun. I fell down some steps outside (always the clumsiest!) but aside from a few cuts and bruises, I had a great time.

Things were fine for a while, but it was always our mum and grandparents who ran around after the three of us. They were there for all of the important events at school or in our extracurricular activities. Peter wasn't involved much at all, and he seemed content that way.

It wasn't long before my parents began to argue all the time. I was just a kid, and sometimes it was scary. Even now, the sound of doors slamming can still make me tense and jumpy.

Once, I was convinced that Peter had hit my mum. I basically dragged Mia down the stairs and out into the front garden. I didn't want her listening to it anymore. I sat her down on the grass and made her promise not to move. We did our special sister handshake so I knew she wouldn't break her promise. That always meant more to her than just saying 'I promise'.

I ran as fast as I could to my grandparents' house for help. It turned out that he hadn't hit her, and I was so relieved. I knew, if he had, that he would never be allowed back into our home or back into our lives, no matter what. They managed to calm everybody down. They were superheroes, my nan and granddad!

After that, there was peace, but only because of the silence between them. We had seen enough to know that was the calm before the storm.

Peter didn't sleep upstairs anymore, and we didn't eat together or do anything as a family. In fact, he barely acknowledged us at all. It was like our house had been split into two halves: my mum, my sisters and I on one side, and Peter on the other. He was there, but he wasn't. He lived a completely separate life.

I remember I was around the age of eleven and they were arguing, which was nothing new by that time. This particular argument was something to do with money, and Peter dropped a pretty big bombshell: "I'm not paying anything for Georgina," he yelled at my mum, "she's not even my kid!" We had recently bought our first computer, and that's where I was when he said it – sat at the computer table, doing my homework. I'll never forget it. Obviously, it wasn't the best way to find out, and I was shocked, but I wasn't as distraught as you might think. Not about him, anyway.

I knew this meant that Megan wasn't really my sister, and that hurt much more than finding out Peter wasn't my real dad. Megan was Peter's daughter from another relationship. There was only a couple of years between us, and as a little girl, she was my best friend.

She was *always* our sister, even when she couldn't come to visit anymore. I was only around the age of seven when I last saw her, and then, it was like she just disappeared from our world. I looked at photographs all the time, and as I grew up, she was always talked about. I felt bad that we didn't get to grow up together – to do things I could remember without being told about it, or a photograph sparking my memory – but it made me happy to know she hadn't just fallen off the face of the earth. She was out there somewhere, and I hoped she was happy.

My mum and Peter soon separated, and he went to live back in his old town. The thread that their relationship had been hanging on to had finally snapped. I think he liked the idea of marriage and the conventional family setting, but he didn't want to make the effort for any of it.

He still had some control for a while. My mum was only earning a basic wage now, and he gave her child maintenance money for Mia, which we needed, so he used that to his advantage. He said he would only give her the cheques if she went out to dinner with him.

It wasn't long before my mum started taking Mia and I along too, and in time, he realised that he wasn't getting anywhere with his soon-to-be ex-wife, and instead, he was paying for four meals every weekend. In time, he gave up and finally just posted the cheques.

You may be wondering about my real father, but believe me, there isn't much to wonder about. I know who he is. He even lives nearby – but he was a sweet-talking, secretly-drug-taking bully, who threatened my mum when she was heavily pregnant, and I have never wanted to know him. I've watched TV shows where people are reunited with an absentee parent. They're happy, or angry, or sad, but they are *always* curious. You can see it in their eyes.

I used to think it was strange that I *wasn't* curious; I don't have questions, I'm not angry or sad, but I came to realise it's because I've always had everything I needed. The only thing I have thought about as an adult is if I have any siblings on his side, how old they are, if they have children themselves, if I'll *ever* know those kind of things… I don't have his surname, so I figure there's just as much chance that they don't either.

Regardless, I just hope he has learnt to be a better person now.

Chapter Four

Whilst my home life was generally happy, my life at school was always kind of tortured. I have atopic eczema, but when I was really little, it was so bad that my body had to be wrapped up in two layers of bandages under my clothes. I was teased for it. They called me names and laughed at me when they caught me literally red-handed, scratching at the patches of bare skin on my hands.

The thing is, I hadn't known anything else back then: having a skin condition was just part of my 'normal'. But in school, it was different. *I* was different, and that wasn't necessarily a good thing.

I was a very particular child too. I guess you could say I had a 'Type A' personality – a perfectionist. I'd start my work over again if I spelt something wrong or made a mistake. I hated crossing things out. Even when we used pencils instead of pens, I didn't like to rub it out because I was convinced the markings were still there. Seeing corrections written in red instead of happy green ticks and gold star stickers made me sad.

Homework had to be done on the day it was assigned, and books had to be read thoroughly, over and over again, until I knew them inside out. Had I not been so insistent on the perfect cursive handwriting, my teachers were sure I could have achieved higher scores in tests and exams – I hardly ever got the papers finished in time!

Later in primary school, I was bullied.

A few girls started it. They'd name-call and whisper about me, knowing I could hear them. They told the other kids not to talk to me. They would pretend to be my friend so I'd think it was over, and just when I let my guard down, they'd laugh at me and chase me away. It went on and on, and over time, almost everybody turned against me. I had no real friends there.

I wasn't physically hurt, but as we got older, they began to threaten me. They kept telling me they'd 'get me' after school, and that was more than enough to frighten me. If it came to that, I wouldn't have known what to do, or how to handle it. I knew nobody there would stand up for me.

Every day, they were relentless and I was vulnerable. Eventually, I told my mum. She went into the school, and the head teacher said he would keep an eye on the situation. Nothing changed. This happened a few more times, but it was always the same routine: the faculty couldn't see anything going on, so maybe I was just acting up, telling her things that were untrue, attention-seeking.

One day, my granddad picked me up. After all the other kids had gone home, he came into my classroom, frustrated with me for taking so long. But when he found me hiding, crying, too scared to leave, he was furious. He shouted at my teacher and then, carrying my book bag and my lunch box in one hand and almost dragging me along with the other, he stormed to the head teacher's office. I'm still not exactly sure what was said, but it was an angry interaction – he was banned from dropping me off or picking me up!

He then insisted on enrolling me into jujitsu classes. We went to a local activity centre and my granddad marched me straight over to the sensei – his name was Neil – and said "I want you to teach her how to hit back." Cowering behind him, I could feel the knots forming in my stomach. "See that kid over there?" Neil said, pointing across the room to a boy about my age, "that's my son. He's a black belt, he has more trophies than anyone I've ever known, he could annihilate anyone who gave him trouble..." I was so scared of the possibility that the bullies would start hurting me like that. If I could just learn to defend myself, if I could show everyone that I was strong enough to fight back on my own, then I'd be okay. It would all be okay. "But he won't do it," Neil told my granddad, "It's not in his nature." He would happily teach me to defend myself, and he did, but he told us that nobody could make me hit back if I wasn't built that way.

It wasn't in my nature either, and we knew it.

Pushed beyond my limits, I cracked. People can only take so much. One day, a girl from my class, Jessica, pushed into me. She was above me on the stairs and had tripped, putting her arms out to stop herself from falling. It was a genuine accident, but I didn't know that. I turned around and said something along the lines of 'don't touch me!' followed by the threat that my mum would find her. I told her my family would get them all. I honestly have no idea where that came from!

The head teacher, of course, having already branded me a liar and most likely considered my granddad to be some kind of crazy hothead, turned it around on me. I told my mum and grandparents what I'd said to Jessica, fearing how much trouble I'd be in with the teachers, not to mention the bullies and the other kids. My mum once again called the school, demanded a meeting and said she was bringing the education authorities with her. This situation was going to be sorted, come hell or high water.

Jessica never seemed to be afraid of anybody, and I certainly didn't scare her, but I wished I hadn't said those things. She wasn't really a perpetrator, but sometimes she was part of it, and that was enough. I was just as frightened of her as I was of the others. My poor mum was rundown, out of options, not sure what to do next. She hit her breaking point too – like daughter, like mother. I didn't know this until after the fact, but she went to see Jessica's mum, Linda. They didn't really know each other, only in passing, but at that point, anything was worth a try. We were all stressed to an unmanageable level. I couldn't continue spending five days a week in that kind of environment, and my mum couldn't continue letting me. Linda promised she would talk to her daughter and try to find out what was really going on.

My mum went into school the next day, off to her meeting, convinced it would be just as useless as the others. She didn't have the education authorities with her, but it didn't matter anyway. The head teacher had claimed to have called them out over the time since we made our first 'allegation'. They had apparently observed the problem, also believing it was a situation that simply didn't exist: a figment of an over-active imagination, just make-believe.

But somebody came forward, they told my mum in the meeting. This person had consolidated my story and proved every single thing I'd said was true. I knew it was Jessica. It turned out that Linda had made her daughter tell her everything. She'd gone into great detail, and the truth finally came out!

Vindication.

After so long, I guess it should have felt incredible, but it didn't feel that way to me. I suppose I was just numb to it, but I was so grateful to Jessica. We didn't become friends overnight, but she backed off and her friends followed. I think the other kids just got bored of it. They probably knew they were being watched even closer now, so it wasn't 'fun' anymore. It was over.

I was so young when I was bullied. I never really knew why it happened, if there was a reason at all. Maybe it was because I was always a bit of a geek. My reading and writing was above average, my homework was sometimes held up as a shining example, and my teachers praised me for my out-of-school achievements. I loved to learn, but I never tried to be better than anyone – I just wanted to do *my* best. I was an accidental teacher's pet. Maybe the other kids were just making fun of me at first, but over time, it spiralled out of control.

All I did in my free time was read, and plenty of those books taught me that there had to be good in amongst the bad – there was a remarkable teacher at my school who had always encouraged and supported me. She kept my young mind as innocent as she could and unknowingly reminded me of the goodness in people. She gave me a hero in a world that seemed scary for a very long time, and I will never forget that.

Chapter Five

Even when it was all over, I continued to be very anxious and very unsure. It was like I was stepping on egg shells all the time, or Monday through Friday at least. I could have easily isolated myself then. I think, if it had been my choice, I would have stayed inside the four walls of my home for as long as I possibly could. I am so thankful for my family, who never would have allowed that, and for my extracurricular activities, for *always* keeping me so busy...

I was one of those super active kids, involved in so many hobbies that I was always being rushed from one place to another. Even though I'm really clumsy, I mastered the science of changing my clothes, eating without spilling and brushing my hair perfectly, all in the back of a moving vehicle.

I was a swimmer, so I did my usual lessons every week and also competed with the local swimming club. I continued with jujitsu for a while. Sensei Neil was brilliant, and I enjoyed being with the other kids there once I'd settled in, but honestly, I became more interested in the vending machines opposite the hall (it was the *only* place that seemed to have white chocolate crunch bars).

I did a bit of gymnastics here and there, and I eventually tried trampolining. I loved trampolining – it was so much fun – but I was constantly injured. It was always me who came down from a jump in the wrong way and ended up with an ankle that was twice its usual size!

I took acting classes too. At some point in my young life, I decided that I was categorically going to become an actress someday; it would force the confidence out of me, and I just loved getting to be somebody other than myself for a while.

After plenty of classes and taking a few exams, I planned to audition for a brand-new theatre company. The thought of it terrified me, but I made myself try as hard as I could. I had a copy of my audition monologue with me all the time.

I pushed through all of my nerves and went to the audition, and I got in!

My family were so proud. Now a member of a new company, I was super excited. I didn't know anybody else who had auditioned, so it felt like a fresh start. Every Tuesday, my mum and I took the train into the city centre and I spent a few hours there, working really hard, learning my craft and having a great time too!

I made a few good friends, three girls in particular. Halloween fell on a Tuesday that year, so we dressed up for our classes, and all four of us turned up as devils!

Some of the kids in the company were more into singing than acting and vice versa. But we all had to do both, *and* a bit of dancing. That was part of the schedule that everybody seemed to dread, except me...

Dancing had been a huge part of my life for as long as I can remember. I'd always belonged to a dance school, and then, in the millennium year, one of my teachers opened her own academy.

My closest friends, my greatest mentors and my favourite memories were all there. Most of us had danced since we were toddlers, progressing onto higher grades together, sometimes because of our ages and sometimes because of our abilities. We made so many memories in classes and rehearsals, and especially backstage during our showcases; running around in tan tights and half a costume, sequins and makeup everywhere, our mothers trying to fix things last minute, everyone stressed and excited, full of adrenaline.

As we got older, we danced most week nights and I was at the academy all day every Saturday. I was so happy when I got the chance to help with the pre-school ballet and tap classes. It was my very first experience working with young children and I loved every second. I know you're not supposed to have a favourite, but I have to admit, I totally did!

But I think I was her favourite too. All the children were wonderful, of course, but there is always one who just touches your heart that little bit more. I'll never forget how she brightened up my Saturday mornings.

Anyway, when our academy was involved in extra projects and performances, or if we were taking our exams, the timetable would be filled with extra classes and rehearsals. We went to performing arts Easter courses and summer schools, we did choreography competitions and all kinds of workshops, on top of our shows. The list is endless, and slowly, my other hobbies faded out in favour of dance.

Lorna, my teacher, prepared my friends and I for a ballet audition once. It was for an adaptation of *Sleeping Beauty,* to be performed on a stage that is grand and beautiful, and pretty famous around here. After the audition process, similar to a rigorous ballet class, we got through. We were so excited. Just to be one of the dancers on that stage after sitting in the audience so many times before, it would be an honour and at such a young age, it was definitely a dream come true.

So, every Sunday, we'd travel to the rehearsal studio and spend hours under the strict direction of a Russian ballet master. He could be frightening without raising his voice, so when he shouted, it could be pretty intimidating. As the performance date got closer and closer, his quest for perfection became more demanding. But nobody gave up, because you'd just think of the endgame – the big picture, the stage, the lights, the applause, your name in the theatre programme. As kids, we didn't have main parts or anything, but a part is still a part.

Carabosse was the ballet version of Maleficent, and as one of her little monsters, I had a darker role to play. It was a new experience for me to be on the bad side, and it was a lot of fun – it was just hard to break the habit of smiling on stage. We got to see the ballerina who was playing Carabosse perform her solos, and she was great. Her dancing was fierce and free, and yet, she remained so elegant.

When the big night arrived, some of us were waiting backstage, watching as another dancer – cast as one of the three fairies – took to the stage. She began to perform her solo, and then suddenly, there was a bang from centre stage, echoing through the wings. She'd fallen and jumped right back up again, carrying on professionally and heroically, still smiling when she was obviously in pain. The ballet director almost roared from the wings. She was probably more concerned with his reaction than her potentially-broken foot!

We rarely got to see the other dancers in rehearsals if we weren't dancing in the same scene together, so I didn't really know her, but I think it all turned out okay in the end. I just remember my heart sinking for her. She was incredible too.

Later in my dancing life, when Lorna told us we were ready for pointe shoes, we were thrilled. I'd taken ballet classes since I was three, and this was one of the great milestones. This was *the* thing to aim for as a ballet girl, especially when you're watching the older students dancing so gracefully on the tips of their toes. After being fitted for our first pairs, we had to sleep in them for a few weeks to break them in properly before training. Soon enough, it was time for our first ballet class *en pointe*.

I'd use the word *wow*, though it's not entirely in the good sense of the word. You're so exhilarated; I guess you don't really count on the pain. Swollen feet, sore toes, snapped toenails, sometimes blood on your foot, the shoe, the tights, the ouch pouch, or all of the above! (Ouch pouches were special gel pads that fitted around your toes and into the front of the shoe. They were miraculous when you tried rising up onto pointe without them, but doing pointe work *with* them was still very painful!)

Dance training was the price of grace and occasional glory. Two of my closest childhood friends moved away from home as preteens, both to study dance at specialist arts schools. No matter what it took, they were always going to succeed. Even at a young and tender age, they wanted it with every bone in their body.

I know, at times, it was more difficult than I can imagine. After all, it's hard enough to start secondary school and make it through those years with the people you have always known. But in the name of success and passion, they were willing to move away, into a world that has always and will always be tough and demanding, with new people, all just as talented and ambitious as they were. They worked hard and devoted themselves to their training, and now, they are both extraordinary.

Learning to dance really was wonderful. Mastering technique took a lot of work, time and practice, and preparing for shows and exams could be undeniably stressful, but it was always worth it. I learnt to be responsible from a young age and to not only take constructive criticism, but to apply it and be grateful for it. I'm also convinced that my extracurricular activities, dance in particular, helped to develop my social skills more than school ever did.

By achieving her own dream of opening an academy, Lorna – 'Miss Lorna' back then – created a huge part of my childhood. We all got to be part of something, and it was something unforgettable. To this day, she remains to be one of the most passionate people I have ever known.

For a long time, dance was one of the only places they weren't. The bullies, I mean. The other place was home. I was never under threat at home, of course, but with Peter still around, arguments often in full swing, and Ellie being in 'teenage trouble' almost every weekend, my house couldn't always promise salvation. Dance was not only safe, but freeing too, and for the most part, everybody got along. Nobody was going to taunt me, and nothing would hurt me. It was never a fearsome place to be. In fact, it could be the perfect distraction – my perfect escape.

Dance was always there for me. When I say that, I mean everything and everybody that encompassed 'dance' – my teachers, my friends, the opportunities we had, the progress we were always making – it *all* helped. Dance helped me to control (or at times forget) the worries I was somehow born with, or had developed with experience.

I was never the best dancer, but that doesn't matter: I didn't have to be. Every time I used my real emotions to perform, I seemed to be praised more. It's all about self-expression. Through studying dance, I also learnt to utilise any creativity I had inside of me. I didn't realise, until adulthood, how prevalent that would be in my life. There is definitely power in artistry.

Chapter Six

As a teenager, my high school friends thought my dancing schedule was completely insane. They couldn't understand why I wanted dance to make up the entirety of my free time, especially when I knew I wouldn't be pursuing it as a career. The thing is, their idea of freedom was different to mine, as was their idea of fun. Most of them liked to hang around on the streets or in parks, but I didn't, and I knew I never would. I heard plenty of stories about how much fun their weekends had been, but I had my own stories too.

In *my* free time, I was having sleepovers with my dance friends. Many weekends, after ballet class on late Saturday afternoons, we would go to a different friend's house. Our pillows and duvets would soon be spread across the floor of the living room, successfully making it look like the cosiest mess ever. We ate pizza and chocolate and watched movies – *Center Stage* being a firm favourite! We talked and laughed and of course, practiced our dances. I'd always be sad to separate with them on Sundays, because it meant Monday was getting closer by the second – Monday at school…

Although my general experience of primary school was pretty tough, at least I knew what it was. Just the thought of going to high school, into the unknown, filled me with debilitating worry. Those stories everyone got told, about the seniors putting the first years' heads down toilets etc., they were *meant* to be funny. You aren't supposed to believe them! It was just something that lingered in the back of your mind if you ever got on their bad side. It gave them a laugh, and it seemed to be some kind of tradition – Ellie had heard the story when she was going into high school, and then she'd laughed about it as a senior.

You're supposed to go full circle and end up as the oldest students, showing the youngest exactly who rules the school, but I didn't see it as comical or harmless anymore, definitely not harmless. I was absolutely petrified. But Jessica and I ended up becoming friends before we went to high school, and I was very happy about that. She was outspoken and feisty and everybody knew it, so I got to hide my insecurities behind her powerful personality.

The other kids knew she was my friend, so they didn't really mess with me. If they did, she fought my battles. Our friendship was generally good, occasionally great, but it wasn't long before I realised something was wrong.

Sometimes, I'd do her homework so she could go out after school. I didn't want to say no when she asked, because I was scared of her reaction. What if she thought I was unappreciative, like her protection didn't matter to me anymore? I couldn't bear the thought. So, even though I barely had time to do my own homework, I just did hers too. It was the easiest option for me.

Also, she would play on the bullying sometimes, and the nerves I'd been left to wrestle with. It was like I owed her, for bringing it to an end, and I truly believed I did. I completed an entire project for her once, as well as my own, and she got a higher grade! My mum found out and she was furious, but I begged her not to say anything.

Most of the time, I had to be home from school quickly to get ready for dance, but she would always take her time. That wasn't the problem, of course – I didn't expect her to rush just because I had plans, but I couldn't walk ahead like most kids probably would. It wasn't that simple. I knew she'd be annoyed at me, and I was always worrying about that. I couldn't risk Jessica turning against me. I didn't want to be vulnerable again. Being a victim in high school would be so much worse than before: bigger school, bigger bullies!

At that time in my life, I used to wet myself a lot too, and it was beyond embarrassing! I'd arrive home nearly always desperate to use the toilet, having walked home with my tummy muscles clenched hard. I was either too late, or I'd only just make it in time. Sometimes, even in those last few seconds, I wouldn't be able to hold it anymore. When it happened, I hoped and prayed that nobody would find out. Nobody who *could* use it against me would ever know.

But it used to frustrate me so much that I'd often find myself in tears. This wasn't 'normal'. I wasn't a little kid who was just wetting the bed anymore, so why was *this* happening, at *this* age? Medically, there was nothing wrong. They just used to say that we never know how much we actually need to use the bathroom until we're almost home. It's like your body knows it's about to experience that kind of relief, so it lets itself go a little bit.

Or, it was my nerves.

Most of the time that this unfortunate incident took place, I'd had a particularly tense or anxious experience. Sometimes, it was just one situation, and other times, the entire day had been spent in concealed fear. Looking back, I'm certain it was linked to nerves. After all, I was always on edge throughout my high school years.

Some days were nowhere near as bad as others, and being busy helped – between school work, dancing, theatre company and spending time with my family, I didn't have a lot of time to think about my fears. I guess they did become less dominant with time, but they were deep-rooted. They could intensify in a heartbeat. Every time a comment was made about me, even if it was a joke, I'd feel the all-too-familiar sense of panic. But it never became more than that. It never became bullying. I learnt that I could take a bit of name calling or the occasional nasty comment because I'd been through worse. Knowing I could get on with my life anyway made things much easier.

Chapter Seven

During high school, you see the cliques forming, kids coming together.

There were the super smart kids, focused, in all the top classes, full of ambition, always on time. There were risk-takers, fun loving, pushing boundaries, doing things they shouldn't do just for the sake of it. There were kids who were always late because of their extracurricular activities, or because they were so unorganised. There were the sport-obsessed students and the kids who purposely forgot their P.E. kits or forged notes from their parents, because they didn't want to go outside in the cold (not helped by the fact that our kits really were hideous!) There were kids who were let off with incorrect uniform or bad behaviour or lateness. That was usually because they had 'things going on at home' – things only the faculty knew about. I worried for them.

Lastly, of course, there were the kids like me: the 'undefined', I guess. They had traits from different cliques, a couple of friends from different cliques, but they weren't part of the clique itself. They fitted in everywhere or they fitted in nowhere, depending on how you look at it. But everybody had their weird quirks and their very normal normalities.

As most kids do, I got to know a whole new bunch of people I hadn't known in primary school. I made a few good friends during those five years, but I don't think any of them knew I was experiencing that kind of fear, and certainly not as often as I was.

My favourite memory of high school didn't even take place in the school, or even with my school friends. It happened at home with Ellie. My science teacher (who was usually such a joker) had been in the worst mood, further exacerbated by our behaviour as a class, even though some of us hadn't done anything wrong. As a punishment, he assigned us an essay on the life of a chip! Yes, I'm being serious – *The Life of a Chip by Georgina Peterson* kind of serious.

I remember my classmates and me looking around at each other, convinced he was kidding and waiting for his face to break into a smile any second, but we were wrong. When I told Ellie, she said I just *had* to let her write it for me, and she wrote the most sarcastic thing I've ever read. It remains to be the funniest essay I have to my name. I was almost too scared to hand it in!

I did manage to have quite a lot of fun in the awkwardness of my adolescence. It was great having an all-female household while I experienced all the usual teenage girl things. My first period arrived a few minutes to midnight on New Year's Eve, and even though I knew it would happen someday, I was mortified. I honestly thought I was dying!

Most of my friends in dance and in school were already talking about theirs, but I still couldn't believe it. My mum and I spent about half an hour in the bathroom that night discussing sanitary options – not exactly the most exciting way to bring in the new year…

Fourteen was a pretty big year for me – first period, first proper experience of alcohol, first injuries (a fractured wrist caused by slipping on conditioner in the shower, a sprained ankle caused by trampolining and a hip disorder caused by something I'm still not 100% sure of).

Most importantly, it was the year that two beautiful baby girls came into my life – my cousin's twin daughters – and I loved them instantly. I knew, from the moment I held them, that I wanted to be more than a random relative they came across at occasional family gatherings. I wanted to be a real part of their lives, so I did.

We have played games, decorated cakes, painted and created things with arts and crafts. We've danced, ran around, watched movies and laughed…a lot. We have spent days together in summer and during their other school holidays. We've had sleepovers, we've made forts and had picnics and barbecues. I went to their Christmas concert to hear them playing piano. I was there in the park when they were learning to ride their bikes. I love going to see them after they've been on holiday, so they can tell me all about it.

As they got older, I started to take them out for their birthday – every year, I tell them we can do anything they want to do, within reason, of course! So far, we've been out for pizza, to the cinema, shopping, had makeovers, found presents on treasure hunts, played crazy golf and other games. But the three of us can have fun doing nothing much at all, and I love that. They have definitely kept my inner child alive and well!

Back in those days, my big sister was always giving me advice. She showed me how to use makeup, even if the stuff she gave me was a good few shades darker than my skin tone. She also taught me how to practice kissing, and she let me borrow her clothes. When Ellie got her first car, we would take drives to pretty much anywhere. We went shopping, out for dinner and to the cinema. We went to the pictures a lot actually, even to rubbish films when we had spare time and couldn't think of anything else to do. She even let me try driving her car once, in an empty car park. I thought I did well, but she says I was terrible at it. She took me to my first ever concert and on the best nights out, before I was even old enough to go.

Ellie would give me instructions and encouragement on the little walk from the taxi to the bar. "You look all grown up and gorgeous, but put your shoulders down." I'd try, but the nerves were rising within me.

"Right now!"

I'd try harder.

"You won't get in if they think you're underage."

"I *am* underage" I'd say.

"Yes, so you're like a rebel, act like one. Shoulders down, big smile, fake it till you make it."

That was her little confidence motto for me, and it did get easier each time. Plus, looking older than I actually was always helped with that fear of being asked for ID at the door. Awkward…

The strangest thing for me to get used to was the attention from other people. The people I knew had their own stories about it, but I never thought *I'd* attract it. I had this image of everybody talking to each other whilst I just stood there, clinging to my sister, frozen with nerves. But to my surprise, it wasn't like that at all.

As I got older, I only really met new people whilst I was enjoying a night out on the town. With other girls, it usually started with a compliment about your clothes or shoes, or dancing to a cheesy pop song together. With guys, it usually began with a flirty interaction, but more often than not, it just ended in good memories, and sometimes friendship. Suddenly, we ended up with a group of friends we only knew from local bars. Killer heels every weekend. Hilarious memories, looking through pictures on Sunday mornings, half laughing, half crying. Occasionally, phone numbers saved into your phone with 'from last night' written next to the name. Most nights out were filled with great stories.

But I soon had to learn that my teenage years wouldn't all be fun and games…

Chapter Eight

My mid-teens also brought a tragedy upon us. It would make stomach cramps, spots and physics homework feel like a walk in the park. My granddad was diagnosed with cancer.

He'd had back pain, but he was *always* working. He had his own woodwork business, but he was also a handy man for basically everyone he knew. The doctors just thought he'd pulled a muscle after lifting a heavy load of bricks, but the pain never went away. During a scan, they found a malignant tumour in his spine, and it was spreading...fast.

He had fought cancer before. I was just a baby, but I'd been told the odds had all been against him. He wasn't supposed to live longer than a year at the most, but he did. He lived thirteen years longer than the doctors ever expected, and he had remained so healthy ever since. He ate well, he exercised every single day, he only drank alcohol on special occasions and he'd quit smoking years and years beforehand. "He will easily fight it again." That's what I told myself when I lay in bed at night, hoping and praying that whatever good forces existed in this world would grant my family another miracle. He did fight, of course: he was a soldier, a hero, a strong contender. He never gave up, but this time, the disease was just stronger. It was stronger than all of us.

He went through every treatment he possibly could. He was taken into hospital for five days, which became a long, tedious and heart-wrenching five weeks. For the last few days of his life, he was comatose. The palliative care nurses encouraged us all to talk to him. "Your granddad knows you are here," they'd tell us, "even if he can't respond."

I sat by his bedside and held his hand – the hands that had worked so hard all his life, the hands that had protected me from danger. I remember noticing that the hand I was holding was his right; the one that had been wrapped in bandages for days after he tried to fix the heel taps onto my new tap shoes, inadvertently jabbing a screwdriver straight through his skin. I'll never forget how many swear words he'd almost said, without actually saying them!

He died on my birthday. It was a sunny Saturday morning.

My grandparents had kept everything I'd ever written over the years. Every time I stayed overnight, they'd buy me a new pad of lined paper, knowing I'd use both sides of every single page in one sitting. So, I decided to write something special for my granddad, something I could use to stand up and tell everybody what he would always mean to me.

I'd been to a few funerals before and had always felt very sad for the people travelling in those big black cars. They were the closest. They were the broken-hearted, and now, I was one of those people. I felt enclosed in the blackness, and I remember feeling so unsettled in the back of the car. Stepping out into the fresh air gave me a moment of relief. The crematorium was filled. It was a real testament to how much he had touched people's lives. Sympathetic smiles travelled back and forth across the room as the service began.

When I stood up with Ellie and Mia to read our pieces, I was already shaking. My bottom lip began to quiver as soon as I opened my mouth. I didn't think I'd be able to get through it without collapsing to the floor in hysterics, but everywhere I looked, there was an encouraging face, and I said everything I needed to say.

The wake was a celebration. We wanted to honour a life so wonderfully lived. My granddad had a great sense of humour and as hard as it was, we knew he wouldn't want us to spend the entire day in tears.

I don't think people ever 'get over' losing someone. We can't. It just doesn't happen. Time helps. Time heals. Time, amongst other things, allows us to move forward. But even time, as powerful as it is, will never give you what you want. The only thing you want is to have them back – that person who was taken from you far too soon.

I thought my granddad would always be there to celebrate our birthdays, to be at my graduation, to walk me down the aisle at my wedding, to become a great-grandfather... I thought he'd see it all. I couldn't visualise a life he was no longer part of, but what I hadn't realised back then is that he will always be part of my life, even without his physical presence.

He was the most influential father figure the three of us ever had, and it still hurts. Even now, there's a twinge on Father's Day, at Christmas, on his birthday and on mine, which is also the date of my grandparents' wedding anniversary. When stories are told, when photographs are found, when a certain type of music is played, when somebody makes a big decision, our loss is still there, as profound as ever.

I've never known exactly what I believe when it comes to the afterlife, but I choose to believe he is with us, with me. I like to think that he can still see us and is hopefully guiding us down the right paths.

Going back to school for my last year, whilst grieving, was an overwhelming experience. I already felt like I'd let him down. High school was a place in which I could and should have excelled, but I didn't. I was good at English, I liked biology class and the artsy subjects. I did well enough, I suppose, but I was too scared to be my best.

I'd prioritised talking and giggling in class with the friends I had made, because, in my mind, that was much safer than sitting at the front listening intently. I was nervous, sometimes beyond belief, and so, I did what I thought was best for me socially, not really comprehending the fact that my grades would suffer for it. I'm not a genius, but I didn't behave badly, so I wasn't really noticed. I guess I was one of the many kids who slipped through the educational gap.

I ended up in a constant state of stress.

I'd go to my dance academy, trying to focus all of my attention on the class ahead of me, but my mind would drift back to the great mass of paperwork that lay all over our dining room table – the essays I had to write, the presentations

41

I had to put together, the revision I needed to do. I was trying to be okay all the time, but everything around me seemed to remind me of the loss I had to deal with, and the emptiness I now felt. Every time I tried to prove my strength, I just felt weaker and weaker.

I spent a lot of time thinking about it, I even wrote pro and con lists – very *Gilmore Girls* of me – and I made a really difficult decision to move on from dance, a hugely significant part of my life.

I missed my teachers and my friends, but more than anything, I missed helping out with the little ones. I also missed dancing, in general, and the freedom it gave me. I'd never known my life without it. I'd never even imagined that I would be leaving the academy someday. After all, I grew up there. Deep down, I knew it was the right thing to do, but that didn't make it an easy choice.

I'll always be grateful to my mum for sending me to dance classes from such an early age, and to Lorna for opening her academy. Being there made me feel safe and distracted from all the bad things, like being bullied, or listening to arguments, or watching helplessly as the most important man in my life was dying.

Years after I left my dancing days behind, I met up with Lorna to ask some questions for a feature article I was writing. She told me if somebody had danced like we did, it remained with them forever, regardless of the paths their lives took, and she was right.

Chapter Nine

When it came to further education, some of my friendships began to dwindle out, including my friendship with Jessica, because we went to separate colleges. I soon came to realise that there was no point studying for my A Levels if I wasn't going to try as hard as I could. I didn't have to be there after all. I could have gone straight into a full-time job.

I chose four A Level subjects and although I enjoyed my studies, I found them all pretty difficult.

I made some friends, including Amy, who was by far my closest friend from high school. I'd seen her around school over the first three years. We knew each other's names, but that was about it, until we were put together in a child development classroom in fourth year.

It was really easy for us to become friends. In college, we started going out to bars together and were often invited to the same parties, especially when everybody in our year was turning eighteen. One of the parties we went to involved a stripper. I remember we could hardly move with laughter, shock and sincere gratitude that he wasn't 'performing' for us. We didn't have to be under the spotlight with that guy. It reminded me of that episode of *Friends* with Danny DeVito guest starring as the stripper at Phoebe's bachelorette party!

I wouldn't say my dreams of acting had completely dissipated, but I certainly became more focused on academia. I wanted to go to university to study English or journalism, or English with a foreign language, or find some kind of course that would allow me to explore all of them.

I had my heart set on a place that demanded really high grades, and I wanted to go there more than anything in the world.

My granddad had praised me for being intelligent, for my love of reading and writing and learning, and he had always wanted me to do something with it. My mum, of course, just wanted me to be happy. She didn't pressure me, but she knew how much I wanted it, and I knew she'd be so proud. I could imagine her three years down the line, all teary-eyed on my graduation day.

I'd been talking about it for so long, and then suddenly, it was time to start applying.

I was open-minded, of course: I looked through other prospectuses and websites, my mum and I went to open days and application advice meetings and so on. But I already knew where I wanted to be for the next stage of my education.

There was a connection, a gut instinct – it just seemed to be the perfect place for me. The university was away from home, but not too far. The literature course I wanted to take looked incredible, but there was a chance to try all kinds of subjects alongside it. They had everything I could ever need right there on the campus. I knew that would be great, especially whilst I was settling in, as I never have been very good with directions or finding places!

We went to the open day, and it just made me more desperate to be there, desperate to start. It was my first choice. You could apply to five places, so I picked four others – safety schools, backup plans – but honestly, I couldn't see myself anywhere else.

I worked myself into the ground, writing and studying and preparing for the exams that would dictate my future, the grades that would hopefully make my dream come true. Even with a weekend job and volunteering a few hours a week, my grades didn't waver. The pressure was definitely on.

Part Two
During

Chapter Ten

The light glares down over me. It's so bright, piercing. It makes my eyes close. I'm more prepared when they open again, and I can see someone at my side. A woman. She's crying, but I can't place her. I can't place anybody and I'm scared. I'm so scared. I don't know what's happening, but I know I'm in pain. It is the worst pain I've ever felt. My head is pounding. My face hurts, and I can taste blood. My tongue feels like it has been ripped along the edges. My entire body feels broken. My muscles ache, all of them, and I'm drenched in cold sweat. No, it's more than that...it's not all sweat... I think... I think I've wet myself! But I'm an adult now! I'm a grown up. What is all this? I don't understand. I wish somebody would just tell me what's going on.

The woman beside me strokes the hair back from my face. Her touch is gentle and comforting, so familiar... I think I know her... Mum? Oh thank God, she's my mum! She knows me. I love her. Tell me what's happening? Please, I'm terrified! You have to help me. I'm so scared...

My vision focuses more when my eyes open once again. I can see people standing around me, above me, concern clouding all of their faces, and I'd never felt so small. I tried to speak; I had to find out where I was, what was happening, what the pain meant and when it would stop. But the words wouldn't come out. I could only just distinguish my mother's voice from another voice, a voice I didn't recognise. A man. The two of them were looking at me, talking to me. I can see their mouths moving, but I can't make out what they are saying. I heard my name being whispered, like a secret. A quiet moment in all the commotion.

Something feels tight around my arm. Wait, I know this place...this is my bedroom! This is my house. These people, they are my family, but they're not the only ones around.

Suddenly, I'm being lifted into the air on a stretcher. I didn't even feel it being slipped beneath my body. Although it was hard and cold, the floor had been strangely comforting, now that I was pretty sure of where I was. But where am I going now? Why have I wet myself? Where is my mum? What is happening? The pain still sears through me. The tears still fall. One of the paramedics smiles at me as they lower me onto the bed in the ambulance. My body flattens until I am horizontal. My mum has found me. She sits close as the same paramedic attaches something to me. I felt the sharp scratch of a needle. I remember she had a kind face. Soon, we were in motion.

An emergency ambulance is a life in danger, isn't it? A life threatened. Their sirens and lights feel like desperation. Desperation to remove the threat, to save that life, to save me. It was my life in danger, but I still didn't know anything. I still didn't know why. My head pounds harder, like it is being struck repeatedly, and my eyes are closing...

Life had been pretty good beforehand. It wasn't perfect by any means, but my grief wasn't as intense as it had been, and as a family, we were 'getting there'. My social life was busy, I'd reunited with some of my friends from dance and I was doing well at college. Things were steady. I was on the right path.

The day had been just like any other. I climbed into bed that night as a typical seventeen-year-old: studying, stressing, working, having fun, planning the future like it belonged to me. But when I woke up hours later on my bedroom floor, my world had been turned upside down. I couldn't communicate. I couldn't even think. I was completely out of control, and since then, I've had to learn what it feels like to have no control over my own body.

It all changed in a heartbeat. No warning, no preparation, no guarantees. When I look back, I wish I hadn't taken my 'normal' for granted, but I guess you'd never know you were taking it for granted anyway. We really don't appreciate what we have until it's threatened, until it's taken away, until it's gone…

After being rushed to hospital, we spent a long time in the Accident and Emergency Department. All I wanted to do was sleep, but I couldn't. Doctors and nurses were in and out of the room, taking my observations and asking questions, primarily to my mother. I cried a lot; with the pain, with the ache I felt from the cannula, and with knowing, somewhere deep within me, that nothing would ever be the same.

The doctors told us that occasionally people can have a one-time seizure. It can happen for a number of reasons including certain illnesses and severe stress. They couldn't make any promises, but we all hoped that was the case. After all, I had been overly stressed, pushing myself way too hard.

I was just so desperate to achieve – to not be mediocre – but this terrified me to the core.

I think it was partly the shock and fear, and partly the pain, that made me feel as if nothing mattered quite as much. But I still had to try. It was May, and my dreaded final exams were upon me. I sat through one of my most important A Level papers, and I cried in silence the whole time.

I'd studied hard for it: I knew what to write in those booklets, I knew all the important statements to make, but they just wouldn't come to me. I was still dazed and disoriented. It had only been a few days since I was discharged from the hospital.

I knew I may never forgive myself, because these grades were make or break. All or nothing. Maybe it would have been easier to handle if I hadn't known the answers, if I'd been unfortunate and very unlucky, getting a paper on the one topic I *hadn't* studied in depth, but that wasn't what happened.

I just couldn't organise the words. My mind wasn't in it. I tried and I did what I could, but I knew then that I wouldn't be attending my dream university.

Chapter Eleven

In July, the midst of an A-Level student's summertime, it happened all over again – the seizure, the aftermath, the same indisputable fear, but this time shattering the possibility of a 'one-time occurrence'.

It would no longer be something I'd escaped from with a few battle scars and a scary story. It wasn't an almost disaster anymore. This, whatever it may be, was definitely here to stay.

After my second seizure, I was sent for all kinds of scans and tests. I was formally diagnosed just after my eighteenth birthday...

I have a really rare form of genetic epilepsy.

I'll tell you more, of course, but first, a little history: the word 'epilepsy' comes from the Greek 'epilepsia' which means 'to take hold of' or 'to seize'. The disorder is noted in Greek mythology, associated with the moon goddesses, who apparently afflicted those who dared to upset them. In the oldest description of a seizure, the person was diagnosed as being under the influence of a moon goddess and actually underwent an exorcism.

A Greek physician, known as Hippocrates, wrote an essay about epilepsy, entitled *On the Sacred Disease*. He accused people of spreading ignorance through an unprecedented belief in dark magic and superstition. He noted the physical characteristics of the 'great disease' and the science behind it. Unfortunately, his views were dismissed and evil spirits continued to be blamed for a really long time. People who had seizures were often grouped together with 'the mentally ill, the criminally insane and those with chronic syphilis' and were subjected to tremendous social stigma.

Although some societies continued to believe that sufferers were cursed, the concept of epilepsy as a medical disorder gradually became more accepted, particularly in Europe and North America. It was in 1857, when a hospital 'for the paralysed and epileptic' was established in London, that people with epilepsy began to be treated on a scientific basis.

I didn't research my disorder until quite recently. I had heard something about how people used to think our bodies were ruled by satanic forces, but I didn't know how true it was that anyone actually believed that! The world used to be a very different place, and I get that, but sadly, even in the developed world, a person may refuse to discuss, or even reveal their diagnosis, due to the stigmas they feel are *still* attached to the disorder. Though we are looked upon as patients, no longer as lunatics, epilepsy is often still cloaked in secrecy and shame. The only real embarrassment, for me, comes with the possibility that I could lose control of my bodily functions during tonic-clonic seizures! But, in general, I've never felt ashamed of my disorder, or of my brain. It hurts, though, to know there are people out there who are still made to feel like that.

The most significant part of diagnosing epilepsy in general is neuroimaging – usually a Computerised Tomography (CT) scan or a Magnetic Resonance Imaging (MRI) scan – to look at the structure of the brain. I had an MRI.

So, there I was, hospital-gowned and horizontal, about to travel into a huge, powerful, tube-shaped machine. They gave me headphones too, because the machine can make really loud noise during the scan.

You can talk to the radiographer through a little intercom, but we didn't talk much:

"Are you okay in there?"

"Yeah."

"Stay as still as you can for me, okay?"

"Okay."

That's how they found all the cells that were affected inside my brain. All over my brain. That's how they first discovered it was not only epilepsy, but a rare form of it. After my blood was taken and sent all the way to a lab in New Zealand, it was confirmed that my disorder was caused by a faulty gene.

When we found out it was genetic, I was referred to a specialist genetics counsellor who helped me and my family to understand. Thankfully, I wasn't the only one who was completely bemused by it all.

I must have looked so overwhelmed with all the information I had to take in, and honestly, I was. So, the doctor explained the neuroscience bits to me by illustrating my chromosomes as cartoon figures – pretty cool, really. We also found out that only about 2% of genetic epilepsies are due to a stand-alone defect, and that's me – I'm a rarity!

Faulty genetic makeup has to start somewhere, and I was hoping it just started with me, but unfortunately, it doesn't. As the disorder is linked to the 'X' chromosome, it had to be with a female. My mum was tested: she has the faulty gene too, but she's not epileptic. On top of the devastation she felt for me, she also carried so much guilt around with her. It didn't matter how many times I reiterated that it wasn't her fault. Seeing her so broken really hurt my heart.

Then, there were my two sisters – same mother, same possibility. The doctors are pretty much convinced now, that this is the reason why my mum miscarried the baby who came between Ellie and me. But, they'd never have checked for *this* disorder. It's too rare, too specific, and there had never been a single sign of it or anything like it, until I had my first seizure.

Ellie and Mia chose for themselves, and they didn't want to be tested. I thought it was the wrong choice at the time, but I was looking at it from my own perspective: I wanted them to be prepared, as 'ready' as they could be, but maybe if they found out there was a definite chance, they would have been too scared to live their lives. I think they were worried enough just watching me go through it.

It was only when Ellie was pregnant that she decided to be tested, more for the potential complications to her baby than for herself. She has it like our mum: the gene, but not the disorder. She had a baby girl, and so the risk remains. We are all descendants of the 'X' chromosome.

I worry about my mum, my sisters, my niece and all of their futures, as well as my own. I'm scared sometimes. We all are, and it's not fair, but that's how it is. We all had to adjust.

Chapter Twelve

The primary treatment for epilepsy is anti-epileptic (or anticonvulsant) medication, and the specific medications prescribed are based on the individual patient. But despite medication, some people (like me) continue to have seizures anyway.

My neurologist started me on one anti-epileptic drug, a low dose, morning and night, but as time has passed, it has been increased. I am now on high doses of two different medications, and I'll most likely be taking these tablets for the rest of my life.

Then, there are the 'extras' – the side effects of my brain disorder:

No driving – a brutal consequence when you have *finally* reached the legal age to learn, and when your cousin *owns* a driving school!

No alcohol.

Stress management.

Pain management.

Hydration.

Sleeping well.

A basic daily routine that I'd stick to.

Always having somebody around.

Modifying the space around me to accommodate the possibility of a seizure.

Every day, week, month and year that comes and goes, these are still our daily concerns. They are just much easier to cope with now, and that comes with time (and a saint-like level of patience)!

Scientifically speaking, during a tonic-clonic seizure, the limbs contract and extend, the back arches, and sometimes, a cry can be heard as the seizure takes hold. The person may bite their tongue, and bites to the side of the tongue are more common in this type of seizure. (Believe me, it's *not* like biting your tongue during dinner)! They may also lose control of their bowels and/or bladder. When the convulsions stop, it usually takes 10 to 30 minutes for the person to return to full consciousness. The period of time is known as the 'postictal state'.

On the outside, that's what people see: the physical seizure.

They see the fall, the convulsions, they may even see a bone break in the midst of it all. One minute I'm fine and I'm vertical; the next thing I know, I'm strapped into an ambulance having lights shined into my eyes and cannulas inserted into my arm, or my hand, or, if my veins aren't co-operating very well, it'll be my foot – and *that* was painful!

My seizures are totally unpredictable. They just attack: any place, any time, any circumstances, no warning whatsoever. They often leave me with pain, headaches, hunger, irritability, fatigue and sometimes an injury, to name a few. I won't tell you how gross my tongue can look afterwards – not to mention how frustrating it is to feel so hungry, but in far too much pain to chew your food, or how I've been so definitively convinced that my deceased grandfather had somehow saved me from smashing my head open on a concrete floor.

I think, for the people around me, it's the powerlessness that gets to them. It's horrible to feel so helpless against epilepsy. Sure, you can give me my rescue medication, and you can try your best to shield my head from danger. You can dial 999 if an ambulance is needed, and you can hope that I'll be okay – I most likely will be. But I'll still be epileptic the next day. I'll still live with the "what ifs" of my disorder, and you'll still jump to your feet when I drop the shampoo bottle in the shower!

(That one is for you, mum!)

The people around me have to see it all the time: me, unconscious, convulsing, then coming into consciousness, usually in severe pain. There have been times when I've stopped breathing, and at least twice that I know of, my family truly thought they had lost me. I can't even begin to imagine that kind of emotional pain and fear.

We all know it *could* be fatal, and that's hard. I know I could fall a certain way, and that'll be it. But we try not to think about that. We don't want to think ourselves into darkness. In fact, I really want to stay in the sun.

The way I feel on the inside – my psychological reactions to being epileptic – are more difficult for people to understand.

I guess I'm a worst-case-scenario kind of thinker. Even as a kid, I tended to think things through and consider all the possible outcomes before I jumped into anything. I've always asked myself questions that began with 'what if?' and then, I was diagnosed. Disability, condition, illness, disease, disorder – whatever you choose to call it, epilepsy is a gigantic uncertainty that I can't get away from. It's within me. But seizures are not my only worries. There are plenty of others.

I'm scared of being disappointed in myself. I sometimes worry about making simple everyday plans because I know there is a chance I'll have to cancel. I worry about making big plans for the future, just in case I'm never able to see them through, because then I might feel like a failure. I'm concerned about my health deteriorating further, and I sometimes worry about my heart (it's possible that this disorder can cause complications there too). I have worried about the effects of my medication and how much medication I'm actually taking.

There is so much to be afraid of.

I mean, I know *everything* in life can be frightening if you think about it hard enough, but knowing that doesn't make it any easier to live with a disorder that hides inside my head.

On the brighter side, I have some super entertaining stories from my time in hospital. I soon began to value my creativity more than ever before, because it always gave me something to do when I was unable to move from my bed. I felt lucky – so incredibly lucky – to have my family around me. But most importantly to me, I have always felt at complete ease with every medical professional I see on a regular basis.

My neurologist in particular is great – so intelligent it kind of baffles me, yet so down-to-earth that you could just be catching up with a friend. I think he has found that balance. He looks at his patients as an entirety: their everyday lives, their families, their hopes and dreams for the future. He takes it all into consideration. It makes a huge difference. He isn't looking at epilepsy: he's looking at me *living* with epilepsy. People often say, "It's you with epilepsy, not epilepsy with you."

Chapter Thirteen

In all the time since my diagnosis, I have had plenty more tests, but the most memorable was my ambulatory electroencephalogram (or my EEG – that's much easier to remember!)

We went into hospital early on a Monday morning, and the nurse plaited my hair back. She then glued multiple wires into my scalp and attached all of them to a brainwave recording device. It was kept safe and dry in a black bag, worn around my waist like a bum-bag. It was hardly Coachella worthy, but good enough for this.

My mum called me her alien child, which was apparently a compliment. Both of my uncles responded to my picture with something like "at least we know you definitely have a brain then LOL!"

I chose to go about my daily life whilst I had my EEG, and if the machine was to pick up on anything that was happening just before a seizure took place, we hoped it was something I'd be able to change. Honestly, it was strangely fun for the first day or so, but I was only sitting at home with my family.

Things changed when we went out the next day. It was my first experience being stared at.

In general, I don't look like I have anything wrong with me. I look 'normal' for want of a better word. It's good because I'm not gawked at constantly, but it can be a hindrance too – people can sometimes judge me a little too harshly. They can't *see* the problem, so it can't be that bad. I think that's the kind of thought process I've been subjected to.

I received a mixed bag of reactions.

Young children looked, but I could tell they were just curious. One little boy came right up to me and said, "Why do you have all those things on your head?" His mum looked mortified but before she could intervene, I smiled and bent down to his level.

"Well, sometimes my brain gets confused and makes me fall over," I told him, "so the doctors put these wires on me to find out why." I was pretty happy with my kid-friendly explanation. He looked interested for about two seconds, then went back to playing with a toy dinosaur.

I told his mother I was epileptic, answering her unasked question. She asked us a bit more about it, and that was that. She wished me well and they said goodbye.

Not bad at all, I thought.

There were people who looked the other way when I caught their eye and parents who told their children to stop staring. There were people who smiled sympathetically and talked to me with a lot of caution and staff in shops who were overly helpful once they had seen my head. People often looked shocked, but I understood. After all, a young woman with a load of multi-coloured wires glued to her head isn't exactly what you expect to see on your daily travels through town.

The only kind of reaction that upset me was rudeness – people who chose to look at me with more insensitivity than curiosity. It wasn't that they were too nervous, or unsure how to act or what to say, they were just rude. They'd kind of shield themselves and their kids from me, like I had some kind of infection they could catch. A few people looked me up and down, shooting me funny looks, like I didn't belong, or at least, that's how their reactions made me feel.

I'd always felt for people with disabilities, even before I was diagnosed. But during that week, I remembered just how much empathy I had for people with visible problems. Although there are a few downsides, it made me feel grateful that my disorder can't be seen on my skin.

During those seven days of my life, I felt like I was living in my own little fish bowl. The thing is, nine times out of ten, people don't mind curiosity. They don't mind questions. They'd rather be asked than be stared at. You can feel concerned, curious, sorry, maybe you're not particularly interested or you're too wrapped up in your own problems, and that is all okay, but there is no room for cruelty. Whether or not somebody looks like you, we are *all* human beings. We should all practice empathy and understanding, over judgement, resistance and closed-mindedness.

It was just my luck (or lack of) that I *didn't* have a seizure that week. It was so frustrating. I'd never wish a seizure on myself, of course, but I'd had so many in the months leading up to my EEG, including a long, violent seizure the night before. I was really struggling, so I hoped I'd have at least one that week, just to take something from it. But nothing. Feeling annoyed, I complained to the nurse who was printing my results out each day. "You'd be surprised how many people this happens to," she said, telling us about a man who had recently said the same thing as me. Then, just as she had removed the last wire, he had a seizure in the chair I was now sitting in.

Part Three
After

Chapter Fourteen

Opening that manila envelope on my A Level results day, I knew I hadn't achieved the grades I needed. Although I still clung to that tiny glimmer of hope, I was prepared. I was ready to claim responsibility for not being good enough or strong enough to fight through it.

By that point, I'd had my diagnosis, and more seizures, and I knew my life was forever changed. The people around me advised me to take time out, maybe just a year, to understand the disorder, to come to terms with it, to accept 'my new life.' But I said no. Absolutely not.

I felt weakened by epilepsy, but I was adamant that my disorder wasn't going to change my university goal. I hadn't done well enough for my dream school, but I figured it was worth trying to get a place at a less-demanding university. So, I became one of the many students calling around in desperation for any places that were still available, and I somehow secured a place on an English course. I'd be studying at a local university, as living at home was now a necessity – completely non-negotiable.

When I told my family, they were so proud, and I was happy enough, but it wasn't the same. It didn't give me the same spark or the same motivation that my first choice had given me, but I had to let it go. A degree, regardless of *where* I studied for it, was better than none.

My seizures increased throughout my first year, but I only had a few on campus. It was horrible enough coming back into consciousness to the faces of those I'd known all my life, so to come back to the faces of strangers was scary. My body was still adjusting to the medication, and so, I often felt zombified.

Second year was much worse. My seizures, now relentless and often violent, meant I was nearly always in physical pain, and I felt scared and on edge all of the time. I was soon paired with a learning facilitator – similar to a mentor – named Anna, and she was amazing to me. But even with her unwavering support, it was so hard to keep up with the workload. I missed so much.

Most of the lectures I did attend either ended up with me being whisked off in an ambulance, or forcing myself to keep my eyes open, trying to listen and take notes, wishing my tiredness came from being out all night, like a 'normal' student.

During the last term of my second year, I rarely passed through the entrance gates. I did all of my work from home. More often than not, I would sit in my pyjamas, exhausted, periodically taking painkillers for headaches and injuries, trying to convince myself that I could get through writing that particular essay. *Repeat after me: I can. I can. I can.* To my great surprise, I passed my modules and was able to progress to my third and final year.

But little did I know, that summer would bring some of the worst hurdles I'd ever had to face…

My seizures occurred at least once a day, sometimes more. I began to count the hours, minutes and seconds without a seizure, rather than days. Even though I was exhausted, sleeping was a battle. I'd wake up in agony with existing injuries, or I'd wake up terrified after a nocturnal seizure, or I couldn't get to sleep through the fear of not waking up in the morning. That's because of SUDEP – Sudden Unexpected Death in Epilepsy. As much as I didn't like to think about it, I knew it was a very real possibility. It petrified me.

It came to a point when I couldn't take a shower or even walk up and down the stairs without needing to crash out. I started collapsing. I'd be sitting down, just talking to my family or watching TV, and my body would just fall. I was severely dehydrated and became a magnet for water infections. My mum kept nagging me to drink more water and diluted juice, and I did, but still, I seemed to stay in a state of dehydration. I'd had about eight courses of anti-biotics and became too weak to visit the surgery, so one of the doctors came out to the house. I collapsed in front of her, and she urged me to go to hospital – a suggestion I'd already been fighting against it. But I gave in.

Stressed, sleep-deprived and unwell, I was hospitalised.

I was hooked up to machines and kept in isolation due to a tummy bug I'd also been hit with. My mum was a godsend. She stayed by my side the entire time, sleeping upright in a chair, keeping in touch with everybody back home, going back and forth when she could. There were times I felt okay in myself, but most of the time, I just felt broken. I felt like epilepsy was in charge of everything now, and that was the one thing I'd always wanted to avoid.

As long as I came back for check-up kidney scans, the doctor finally said I could go home, and I was so relieved. But my family soon noticed how awful my moods were. My feelings became very intense. I'd be okay, but then something would come over me, dragging me down in an instant. I cried a lot and so often wanted to be alone. That wasn't like me – I'd never been a huge fan of my own company.

I remember wishing for 'before' – wishing for the girl I used to be. She was bubbly and fun-loving, always smiling. She had goals and dreams and plans – a life plan. But she failed, and this version of you is just a product of her failure. *You're a shadow,* I told myself over and over again, s*tupid, ugly, useless, boring, pathetic, a freak…*

We are in our own heads all the time, and I managed to convince myself that I was worthless. *You're a burden to your family. They only love you out of obligation. You say you love them and you'd give your last breath for their happiness, but you are the reason why they are unhappy. You're miserable, you ruin plans and you break every promise, you take everything to heart, you make mountains out of molehills.* Silent insults were always hurled out of the angry voice within. I became numb to it, and soon, I felt nothing.

The next time I had an appointment with my neurologist, I was very quiet, but my worried mother explained things from her perspective. He suggested and encouraged me to talk to a neuro-psychologist, a colleague of his, reiterating that she would be able to help me. Nothing was changing, so I agreed to meet with her.

She asked me questions, and we had a good talk. She referred me for an intensive course of Cognitive Behavioural Therapy and set up a pre-treatment phone consultation with one of the therapists. But during the time in between, I hit rock bottom.

Chapter Fifteen

I tried to kill myself.

The odd thing is, I didn't really contemplate suicide. I didn't make plans, or think about my funeral, or write letters. I wrote notes to my family once, but that was through the fear of my disorder killing me, not the fear of taking my own life. I wasn't living. I was simply existing, and that was never going to be enough. I couldn't bear the thought of spending my days like this forever – scared of everything, burdening everybody, only the voice in my head to keep me company when I was alone.

I'd given up on myself. Totally and completely, and I didn't care. I wasn't worth saving. That day, when the house was all mine, and I pushed the pillow down, hard onto my face, trying to stop myself from breathing, I couldn't tell you the thoughts that were racing through my mind. In fact, I don't know if I was thinking at all. I was just... numb.

It was only when my sister came home, into my bedroom and startled me out of my own headspace, that I knew this was all wrong: it was never supposed to be this way.

My family were beyond distraught. I'd never seen so much hurt. But despite the wreckage I'd brought upon us, it made me realise: I loved them more than I hated myself. I always had. I always would. They *were* the light, and that became my first step.

I went ahead with the phone consultation later that week, and the therapist asked me about self-harm and suicide. I wanted to lie, to pretend it hadn't happened, to block it out and never speak of it again. But my heart told me I had to be honest, and I followed it.

I had my first diagnosis of clinical depression.

Depression really is like a thief in the night, striking when you are the most vulnerable a person can be. I felt so lost and unstable, not just in my life, but in my own mind. It consumes you, and one day, you just won't recognise yourself. Suddenly, you're not who you used to be.

From there, therapy came around very quickly. Soon enough, I was also diagnosed with an anxiety disorder. Epilepsy, depression and anxiety became a triple threat. They had formed a chronic grip on everything that was once mine. But it was time to fight back, as hard as we could. I just wanted to be happy, and for that, I needed my life back.

I was overly apprehensive, truly believing that nothing would get me through this. I'd have to feel this way forever because I was stupid and I'd already taken it too far. But I was wrong, and over twelve traumatic weeks, I began to feel like a changed woman. The sessions were a lot more challenging that I could have anticipated: there were plenty of tears, a lot of panic, shaking and fidgeting, but by the end, my outlook on life was more positive than it had been in a long time. My desperate, drastic action almost felt like it was in another lifetime.

I'd been trying so hard to pretend I *hadn't* tried to take my own life, but I couldn't. Still, to this day, it was one of the hardest things I've ever had to face. Only my closest family members and my doctors knew about it. I talked about it in great depth with my therapist, over and over, through and through; my disordered emotions alternating between fear, guilt and overwhelming sadness.

But in time, I was able to leave it there. I left it behind, in the past where it belonged, and I didn't breathe another word about it for a very long time.

Chapter Sixteen

I felt so much better in myself, but there were still cracks beneath the surface. There were certain things that could drag me all the way back down, and university was one of them. I'd mentioned it a few times, but my family kind of shrugged it off. They thought it was just a statement I threw out in the heat of a tense moment, especially considering the state of my mental health.

I had a seizure that wasn't particularly bad compared to some of the others I'd experienced, but when I came around, I just cried and cried. Sobbing in my mum's arms, I told her I didn't want to go back, and I was serious. I just couldn't do it anymore. There was no way I could manage to keep up now. I'd rather quit, than try my hardest and end up failing. Failure had always been one of my greatest fears. "But all that work will be for nothing if you leave," my mum protested, when we discussed it calmly. I told her I'd fail my final year anyway, so either way, it would be for nothing. If I decided to quit, it was my choice. I wouldn't be a successful graduate, but at least I wouldn't have to be embarrassed.

Student loans, stress, my poor mum having to take time off work to drive me there because I couldn't face public transport anymore, the anxiety, the headaches I'd suffered for weeks after banging my head on the desks and floors during my seizures – it was *all* for nothing. I wouldn't have anything to show for it anyway, so I might as well spare myself the shame.

She caved in eventually. "If this is what it's doing to you," she began, "well...I'd rather you were healthy...so...I'll be fine with your decision." More than anything in the world, my mum wanted me to stay as 'better' as could be. My disorder couldn't be cured, but she wanted me to be able to manage everything else; to stop panicking and learn to relax, but she certainly wasn't 'fine' with my choice to leave university.

I knew that because I wasn't happy about it either. Two out of three years completed and I was throwing the towel in. It wasn't what I wanted, but I just couldn't go back. I didn't tell the university or even Anna – I kept putting off the phone calls and then, somewhere along the line, I ended up stationary shopping for my third year. I didn't know exactly when it had happened, or how I didn't notice, but I was subjected to a bit of reverse psychology from my family, especially my mum. Somehow, she had sneakily convinced me into going back. I was going to push through my final year, and I was absolutely going to get that degree!

Of course, a surge of new-found motivation and a box of my favourite pens didn't make it easy. In the first couple of weeks alone, I had around twelve seizures on campus, and the number continued to rise. My mum started waiting around in the car park or the coffee shop, ready for someone to call, and she'd be there, quite literally picking me up off of the floor. Soon enough, the faculty advised me to do my work from home again, whilst they made a more secure, less dangerous plan for me. It couldn't continue this way.

Safety first and education second, it took seven weeks until I was allowed to go back.

Everything had changed. Instead of the usual lectures and seminars, I began having weekly one-to-one tutorials in a student counselling room that was basically empty – free of anything that *could* be a potential hazard. There were three chairs: one for me, one for the tutor and one for Anna, and that was it.

One-to-one tutorials may sound perfect to the struggling student – I'd have the full attention of the teacher so I'd learn more, which is true in a way, but my time was cut drastically short. Each week, we had to cram two lectures and two seminars into a one-hour time slot, sometimes less, depending on their schedules and the unpredictable state of my health. I was taking four separate modules every term, so instead of sixteen hours a week in academic study, not including library study, tutor meetings and group projects, I had four. Just four hours a week.

I often had to cancel because I was in hospital, or because I'd had multiple seizures the day before and could hardly function enough to brush my teeth, not to mention focusing on intense final year Literature studies. I did a lot of work from home and communicated with my tutors via phone calls and emails, when one or both of us couldn't be there. I was so appreciative of their understanding and patience. They had seen first-hand how suddenly my disorder could hit. After all, I'd collapsed into seizures many times, right in front of their eyes.

I had worked out from each of my separate results that my degree classification would be a 2:2, and I was okay with it – I had to be – but I was disappointed too. Everyone around me was telling me how fantastic it was 'considering the circumstances'. But to me, my circumstances were no excuse.

A month later, I received another manila envelope, with the university logo and the words 'do not bend'. I knew it was my certificate. It was what I had to show for my last three years in education. You can imagine my joy when it read: *"Bachelor of Arts with Honours in English, with Second Class Honours – Division One."*

I had earned the second highest classification. I had a 2:1!

Typically for me, I started to panic, just in case it was the wrong result. I even called the university to make sure. But there was no mistake. They'd got it right! The certificate I was holding was completely correct, and I could finally let my pent-up tension dissolve into excitement. It was the first time that I'd felt truly proud of myself.

But I wasn't finished with university yet: I still had my graduation day. I chose not to take part in the usual summertime ceremony. I wasn't well enough: my seizures continued to be relentless, and I knew I'd be in fear whilst walking across the stage, in amongst all the students I'd been isolated from.

Most of all, that ceremony was coming up really soon, and I just wasn't ready. I needed more time, and I had the chance to take it. Luckily, the part-time students would be graduating in December and I was granted special permission to attend that ceremony instead. I'd have time to relax, to re-evaluate and to figure things out.

Day by day, time seemed to pass slowly, but when December arrived, it felt like I'd only finished my finals a few days ago. I'd ordered my cap and gown, my family had taken the day off work, and we were going out for a celebratory dinner afterwards. I was okay at first, even a little excited. We collected my cap and gown, and we started to take some pictures, but suddenly, I felt funny.

My legs felt like they were buckling beneath me. I was too hot and beginning to stumble over my words. Panic took hold. I just couldn't do it. I couldn't face the ceremony. We talked to a member of staff, and she was so nice about it. She let me look at the hall, to see if it made me feel any more at ease, but it didn't. The grandness of the place and the image of so many unknown people in the auditorium made me feel so much worse. Despite the disappointment I felt in myself, I had to back out of the ceremony.

When I felt a little calmer, safe in the knowledge that I wasn't being forced to participate, we went straight through for the professional photographs. (I still prefer the ones we took ourselves, but that's okay.) Just before we left, my mum took the traditional picture of me throwing my cap into the air. Ellie and Mia were messing around, making me laugh, and I have a huge smile on my face. That meant more to everybody than watching me walk across a stage riddled with anxiety.

We went back to the car, and as we started to drive away, I watched the place getting smaller. I didn't have the typical university experience. Those three years were harder than they ever should have been, but seeing the smile on my mum's face, my sisters trying on my tassel hat and hearing my nan tell me how proud my granddad would be, I knew it was all worth it. Pride just radiated from my mother. She ordered the best package from the graduation photographers, then she framed my picture and my certificate together, hanging them up in our home.

To others, it's proof of academic achievement. But to me, it's proof that I didn't give up on myself and a reminder that I never should.

Chapter Seventeen

After graduation, I made a plan. I didn't have a focus anymore, and I didn't want to just sit at home day after day, dwelling on all the things I *couldn't* do. I wasn't ready to get another job just yet, but I wouldn't allow myself to drift back into a depressive state, and so, I decided to devote my new-found time to volunteering. It always feels good to give back.

Having worked with young children since I was still a child myself, that was the obvious choice. I started working as a classroom assistant at a local primary school, and I loved it. I thought about that one teacher in my primary school and how much she had impacted my childhood and my life. For now, I was just a volunteer, but I figured I could still have some kind of impact on these kids. I worked with five and six year olds, and I had the chance to read with them on a one-to-one basis. That became my favourite part, because I could really get to know each child as an individual, rather than in a sea of thirty kids in a classroom, all competing for the teacher's attention. I remember seeing their eyes light up when I praised them for getting something right, and those moments when they finally just 'got it' – whatever it was they had been struggling with – they were the best moments.

I received a lot of compliments on the job I was doing, and I settled in quickly. My disorder had been explained to the staff in detail and to the children in a way they vaguely understood. I knew it would happen at some point, and I wanted them to be as calm and unaffected as they could be. The first seizure I had at the school was near the office, not in front of the children. One of the teachers called my mum and an ambulance. Another teacher came to my house a few days later with a card and a huge bouquet of flowers. She told me the children had helped to arrange them. It was such a lovely gesture, and I felt so lucky that my disorder wasn't going to be an issue there.

Their encouragement made me believe I could actually progress to being a teacher someday.

As time went by, I had more seizures; in the classroom, in the staff room, outside, even in the toilets. I didn't go in when I was unwell, which wasn't often, but I knew being ill could increase my chances of having a seizure. Missing a day still made me so anxious, but they always understood, reassuring me that it was the best thing to do. I developed more confidence in my ability to connect with children, just in time for my second venture into volunteering.

I was just about to celebrate my 21ˢᵗ birthday when I finally became a volunteer on a children's ward at the hospital. I couldn't wait to start. The application process was long and quite rigorous. I had told every single person I came into contact with about my disorder, because I knew I was going to love working there, and I didn't want to start this journey if my seizures would be a problem. But, luckily for me, they didn't view it as a problem either.

My credentials for working with children were fairly strong, and in fact, my determination to lead a good life *with* a disorder, had worked in my favour. One woman even said to me during my final interview that the hospital was, after all, the best place to be if I was going to have a seizure.

When I was finally accepted onto the voluntary programme, it felt incredible. Things were definitely looking up!

I started on a Monday morning. It was a new week and a new beginning. I went to bed as early as I could the night before. I was very nervous, but excited too and just hopeful that I'd do well in whatever role they had decided to give me. My mum took me to the hospital and a woman met me at reception, introducing herself and walking with me to pick up my t-shirt and have my picture taken for my photo ID. She was nice. She told me I'd been placed as a ward buddy and I was ecstatic. Working directly with the children was exactly what I'd wanted.

She took me up in the lift and showed me into the ward, but the first member of staff we spoke to had no idea who I was or what I was doing there, never mind that I came with medical baggage of my own. The next member of staff showed me around in a rushed manner with very brief details about the problems these kids were facing – kidneys. That was pretty much all I knew about it.

There were two sections on the ward, but I would be working with the children on the other side of the double doors. They were on dialysis – renal failure. I could have burst into tears as I met each of the four children, sat in huge chairs, tables in front of them, relatives opposite them, nurses rushing back and forth to the machines they were hooked up to. But I plastered a smile onto my face and held it together. I took my cues from them, and I became strong.

"Err…do you think you could work with these children today?" the chaotic woman asked.

"Of course," I replied, and so it began.

I sat down with the littlest girl first. Ava was five, but frequently pointed out that she was nearly six. We drew pictures and talked about the Disney channel. In fact, we talked about all things Disney! Her favourite princess was Jasmine and mine were Cinderella and Belle (I couldn't choose)! Her eyes lit up, as I'm sure mine did too. Disney will always be magical. I also started talking to her mum. I could tell she was a little cautious, and our conversations were slow to begin with, but that didn't last long.

I knew I wanted to be somebody that these parents could put their trust in. Maybe I'd be able to provide them with even the smallest of breaks – just a chance to breathe.

Another child, Joe, was always either on his games console or texting his friends. He was around thirteen, so I knew that would most likely be the case. I always checked if he wanted to do something I could help with, and he always said 'no, thank you.' But one time, he asked if I'd heard about a new video game that had just came out. I shook my head as

I sat down, wishing I'd actually listened to my sister's ex-boyfriend when he talked about the x-box. Anyway, Joe's parents had promised they could pick it up when he'd finished on dialysis for the day. He explained it to me, and for all I knew about gaming, he could have been speaking a different language, but I listened intently anyway. I couldn't help but smile – just the fact that something could still bring him joy whilst he was going through something so terrible. At the end of our conversation, computer games sounded like fun, even to me.

There was another teenager there on my shifts too – Leah. She was lovely and very polite, a great kid really. They all were. She was extremely quiet, but her mum was very talkative, so I still learnt a lot about their family and what they had been through. It was difficult, to say the least, hearing her tell me about Leah becoming ill. I hadn't asked her to tell me – she just started to talk about it, and I was happy to listen to anything they said, including all the devastation. It makes us human. As wonderful as it is to be happy, we can't always feel that way.

I looked into her eyes, seeing my own mother and all the qualities that make parents so undeniably strong. I hoped she had somebody looking after her whilst she looked after her daughter. That's important too.

Then, there was Emily. She was nine, and although each child gave me so much more than they'll ever know, she probably impacted my life the most. She changed me for the better. I got to know her parents well, and they got to know me. They were incredible.

When I spent time with Emily, I could look at the world in a whole new light. It's rare to have an immediate bond with anyone – adult, child, male, female, happy, sad – but I had it with Emily. We worked on little projects together, and they were full of creativity and hope. We had matching princess bracelets from a children's magazine. I made everything as fun as I could, and I made sure her parents knew I was there for them too. I always tried to get the balance right.

Chapter Eighteen

But there was something none of them knew. It was going on in the background, behind the scenes, and would soon overshadow the joy I had found – the staff.

Some of the staff members on the ward would pull me aside about anything and everything, or at least, that's how it felt. For example, a conversation with a parent in which they had overheard a mention of my disorder. They told me I couldn't put my own problems onto these poor parents who already had so much on their shoulders. They didn't let me explain that the parent had directly asked me a question about it.

Surely, they didn't expect me to shut them down, to say I couldn't discuss it, to look into the eyes of these mothers and fathers whose trust I had gained, who openly discussed their children's health with me, and seriously answer with the words 'I can't tell you'.

I was pulled aside for drinking water in front of the children, because they weren't allowed to drink a lot on dialysis. I apologised, but I tried to explain that I had to stay overly hydrated for my health. Another time, Emily's parents and I talked about a medical documentary that had been on TV the night before. I was pulled aside for that too – they wanted me to be careful what I said, to think before I spoke, because I could be giving them 'false hope'.

It wasn't that kind of conversation, but I found myself unable to explain. I kept getting too nervous and tongue-tied, but honestly, they didn't give me chance to explain anyway.

Ava asked me for some toast once, so I asked a member of staff if I was allowed to do that. Being a volunteer, I wasn't exactly sure. She answered me, but she made a comment about how I should already know what I was and wasn't allowed to do. I would have understood if they'd given me rules or instructions on my first day and I just hadn't listened properly, but that didn't happen. I had to go with my instincts, but for my own state of mind, I *needed* to check the things I wasn't absolutely certain of.

For me personally, one of the worst things they said was that I wasn't splitting my time equally between the children. But the thing is, only two of them actually *wanted* to do activities with me. The other two were teenagers, and I still interacted with them, of course, but they just wanted to do their own thing, like most teenagers do. By that point, I was always stressed and full of nerves, overthinking every word I said to everybody during my shifts.

My head felt too heavy for my shoulders.

Deciding to leave was one of the toughest decisions I made. The last thing I wanted to do was leave the kids. It broke my heart and I knew it would, but I didn't feel like I had much choice. I could stay until they actually got rid of me, then the decision wouldn't be my fault, but I knew that wasn't going to happen. They'd have to find a real reason to dismiss me – something I said that I couldn't explain, something I did that I couldn't deny, something I *wouldn't* be able to appeal against.

Their issues were either unprecedented, taken out of context or I just wasn't given the opportunity to explain. I wasn't perfect, but I did the best I could. With no real preparation or guidance, I thought I was doing pretty well.

The other option was to leave, whilst my good memories of being there hadn't been completely tarnished. I no longer looked forward to my shifts, and my stress levels were off the charts.

Maybe I was paranoid, but from the things they said to my face, I feared that the staff were talking about me when I wasn't around. My mum was so angry, trying to calm me down as I cried all the way home, knowing that was it. I wouldn't let her make a complaint. I promised I'd write a letter once I felt calm and level-headed again. I did write that letter, but I've never sent it.

I want you to know, the staff were certainly not nasty people. They wouldn't be in that kind of career if they were. They do an incredible job, and I'm absolutely sure that they never had the intention of upsetting me. But at the same time, I was clueless as to why it didn't work out for them. Maybe I wasn't as good as I'd thought. I have no idea, but maybe, it just wasn't the right time.

From the moment I met those children, they opened my eyes. I hoped and prayed for them – I still do and I always will. I just wish I could have had the chance to explain to their parents, that under better circumstances, I never would have disappeared from a child's life. I wouldn't have been there one day and gone the next. Had I not felt forced out, I would have been there for them as long as they wanted me to be. It still deeply upsets me sometimes to know I'll never get that chance now.

I'll never forget any of them and how inspiring their bravery was to me.

I was devastated, and I couldn't bear the feeling of failure, but I continued working at the school. I tried to do as much as I could, hoping to increase my hours and progress as far as I possibly could. I was still having seizures regularly, some in front of the children, who were always great with it – kids are so resilient. I remember they used to place cushions all around me, and when I came back into consciousness, they'd make sure I was okay. It was really sweet. One little girl even wrote me a checklist to make sure I was eating, drinking, taking my medicine and sleeping, telling me, "it will make you better."

But over time, I noticed things beginning to change.

The teachers didn't include me as much, with the children or during breaks in the staff room. The atmosphere just seemed cold, and it was unsettling. They stopped praising me, as they always had before, and so, I started to panic. Maybe I wasn't doing my best anymore. "Maybe I'm just not good at working with children anymore," I'd think to myself when I was in bed at night, wondering how I could turn it all around.

I raised my game and tried to go above and beyond my role, but it wasn't long before I knew I'd be out of there. It was happening again.

After another seizure, I was picked up and taken home. I'd hurt myself and I was absolutely exhausted. I went straight to sleep.

During that time, the head teacher called my mum, telling her they couldn't keep me there anymore; that the seizures were too frequent and too difficult for them to handle. They said looking after me was taking away from teaching time. My mum, angry and upset for me, told them it was unfair. She'd seen it with her own eyes – the school was open-plan, so when I had seizures, the teachers and other assistants would hear all the fuss, and they would come out of their classrooms too. At first, it was out of pure concern. They'd be panicked and worried; some trying to help me and some trying to keep the children focused on other things. But now, when my mum came to pick me up, often meeting the paramedics there, some of the staff were just stood around, having a chat and drinking cups of tea. "She only needs one person to protect her head," my mum said to the head teacher, "she's unconscious, it's not her fault that your staff crowd around her." But it was no use.

Their minds were made up, and that was that.

It was a tough time. I'd never claim to be an angel, but I'd always liked to help other people. That's why I was so happy to help out at my dance academy at a young age. That's why I volunteered to read and write with younger kids in high school who struggled with literacy. I was brought up with a strong work ethic, and I had my first paid job when I started studying in college.

Now, I wanted to work voluntarily. I just wanted to help. I wanted to make a difference, and even though everybody knew about my disorder and what it entails, nobody seemed to be empathetic, not when they stopped feeling sorry for me anyway. They were all quick to be berate me if I did something wrong, and yet, nobody seemed to credit me for trying as hard as I could.

Chapter Nineteen

Life certainly wasn't going the way I wanted it to. After I'd failed at volunteering, I sat at home day after day, on a downwards spiral. On top of my continuous anxiety and overwhelming mood swings, I began to feel jealousy – strong, consuming jealousy. But I wasn't jealous of millionaires who lived so luxuriously, or celebrities who always seemed to look perfect. Everybody wants those things sometimes.

Instead, I was envious of everybody around me: everybody who had everything I'd envisioned for my life, but could no longer have. Everybody who could just do standard, everyday things without a second thought, because in my eyes, they took it for granted. My life had to be very carefully lived, and I couldn't do anything with ease.

My most intense experiences of jealousy have definitely been towards my sisters; at different times, in different situations and often for different reasons. I tried to tell myself over and over again that there was no need to feel the way I did. We each had our attributes and our flaws. None of us were superior or inferior to the others. But, it was no use.

There were times I was certain that they not only believed they were better than me, but that they also revelled in it. I convinced myself that they found joy in being prettier, thinner, smarter, funnier, happier and healthier than me. Just once, I wanted to be pretty. Just once, I wanted to be 'the fun one'. But most of all, I so desperately wanted to do the simple, most trivial things I watched them do every single day. Jealousy was really hard to handle.

All I could see in Ellie and Mia were their qualities; the things that made them so unlike me, the things that made them so perfect. I confided in my mum, and she could have spent forever telling me that it wasn't true, not to be stupid, to stop bringing myself down, but I believed I was just being honest. I was being real. I was just saying what everyone else was thinking.

I even remember thinking I'd never find a partner, because as soon as they met my sisters, as they inevitably would, I'd be forgotten.

I always try to keep in mind that there are people in this world whose lives are much harder than mine, but Ellie and Mia became constant reminders that people also had it much easier. Had I been in a rational state of mind, I would have seen the situation clearly, as it was, rather than how I viewed it – they had faults too. Their lives were not perfect and neither were they. I had been resenting them for the things that neither they nor I could control.

For example, I hated that they could take a quick shower, because my showers took so much time and left me exhausted. I had to use prescription scalp treatment because of my eczema. I couldn't use any nice soaps – they all had to be unscented, free from anything that could set off my oversensitive skin. I had to follow a special skincare routine after my showers too, and it drove me mad because it took so long.

Rationally, I know that the way I had to shower wasn't my sisters' fault – obviously! – but in the moment, frustrated and upset, you just don't think that way. Rational thoughts are non-existent. You *can't* think straight, and everything became a struggle.

When Ellie's life moved on, I started to feel jealous in a completely different way. It wasn't about how she looked or what she did anymore – it was about sitting on the side-lines watching her be happy. She met someone, they moved in together and she fell pregnant. I didn't want all of that, and certainly not yet, but I felt like I was watching my sister thrive as I remained stuck. She was independent, she didn't burden anyone, and she could do anything she wanted. Mia could too, but her life hadn't moved on yet. She was still in preparation to move forward, and I didn't want that to happen. I was supposed to do everything first, before her, because that was the natural order. But my little sister would overtake me someday, and I couldn't let her leave me behind.

Mia and I had started to develop a great friendship, and it surprised us both, considering we'd never been able to get along for more than a couple of hours at a time before. We had very deep heart-to-hearts alongside our silly, laugh-out-loud conversations. We talked about the TV shows she watched, partly because they were her undeterred obsession, and sometimes because that's how she told me her real feelings. So, I always listened, just in case there is some kind of hidden message.

I often talk about the person I used to be, because I feel like she missed it. She was so young when I was diagnosed. I wanted to make sure she knew that I wasn't always this way, and that I didn't mean to inflict her childhood with my problems and my selfishness. Mia doesn't resent me – she understands. But I still felt bad. I wasn't the big sister I wanted to be for her. I didn't give her everything that Ellie had given me. I couldn't drive her around, or give her advice on certain things, because I hadn't experienced them either.

Mia says I'm the strongest person she knows, but she is a big part of the reason I try to be brave. They both are.

I soon came to realise that, regardless of how much time it took, I would eventually move forwards too. But I'd forgotten that 'moving on' doesn't have to mean moving out, or getting married, finding your perfect job or having babies. It's just about moving on from where you are today – right now – and taking even the smallest steps forward. Ellie moved on from her old life in order to start living her new one, but she never left us. She never left me, and she never will.

It always felt so strange, to love and trust them as much as I do, but to resent them at the same time. They were everything I couldn't be, but they were not to blame. Nobody was.

I'm so glad I managed to solve the puzzle of my envious emotions, because it would have eventually driven my sisters and me in three different directions, and it would have been my fault in the end.

Plus, our big sister moving on in her life gave us the new title of 'Auntie'. I was ridiculously impatient from the day I found out she was pregnant. I had her due date on a countdown, and once she had reached it, every day began with a wish that 'today will be *the* day'. Eight whole days after her due date, Ellie finally went into labour, and I was beside myself. Today really would be the day. I spent the day with my phone attached to me, looking at it every few seconds, even though it hadn't made a sound. The day seemed to go on and on, like it was endless, until 5:30 p.m. when my mum called.

She was here. My niece had arrived. I could hear her cries in the background, and I already felt so much love for her. I talked to my sister on the phone and cried telling her how proud I was. She was so overwhelmed. They stayed in the hospital overnight, due to the freezing winter night that was upon us, and I barely slept. I kept scrolling through the same five pictures my mum had sent to me. Lilly was beautiful. Lilly *is* beautiful.

I couldn't suppress my excitement the next day, knowing I'd be meeting her soon. But devastatingly, I have no memory of meeting my precious niece for the first time. I'd started having complex-partial seizures (more commonly known as absence seizures) on top of my usual tonic-clonics, and they scared me. I wasn't accustomed to them yet, and they had started to bring on panic attacks too. Occasionally, I lose the memory. Sometimes it comes back, sometimes it doesn't, and unfortunately, our first meeting has never returned. Not so far. I have pictures, of course, and the first video I took of her, but more importantly, I have an infinite number of memories since then.

My niece is so clever and funny and absolutely perfect. She is my littlest friend and my biggest motivation.

Chapter Twenty

Ellie turned thirty a few months after Lilly's arrival. She decided against a big party – a decision I was secretly relieved about – and instead, we went on a family break, away from all of our daily lives. We stayed in the U.K., and it was a place we had been to as kids. It was so peaceful, and I was really looking forward to it.

Despite the excitement I felt with Lilly, I wasn't in a great place emotionally, but this trip helped me to refocus. It was full of wide open spaces, nature at its finest: huge grassy fields, mountains that seemed to reach the sky, elegant flowing lakes.

My definition of beauty was sometimes materialistic. The modern world does that to people. I thought about my appearance all the time – the number on the scales, the clothes that were in fashion, my desperation for flawless skin, trying to be the perfect woman… But during our break, as cutesy as it may sound, 'beauty' was just the way the lake looked in the sunshine.

I'd never seen things the way I was now. I hadn't realised how perceptive I'd become, perhaps ever since the day of my diagnosis. I was a different person now. I'd progressed in some ways, but regressed in others, and on my darkest days, I really did feel like a shadow of the girl I used to be. I was living in the grip of anxiety and bouts of intense sadness that crept up on me. I also lived in total fear of my seizures. I'd been trapped for so long in a world that gave me nothing but negativity.

The worst part of this horrible world? I was its creator.

Back at home, I thought about my family and how incredible they were to me, especially my mother. My struggles became hers too, and through them, she became one of my best friends. My mum, my sisters, my nan, my niece, my uncles and aunties and cousins – they all loved me. Some people aren't so lucky. Some people are all alone, and I was surrounded by love...

But you lose yourself when you're ill like that. Mentally, I mean. You forget who you are and what you have. I was focusing too much on who I *wanted* to be and what I *didn't* have. I'd spent so long beating myself down. I couldn't remember the last time I felt okay in myself.

I made a promise that I'd look through every single piece of paper I'd been given in CBT and in counselling. My plan was to become my own therapist, kind of. I wanted to look after myself more, and to stop allowing my disorder to make me so unhappy. Epilepsy will always be part of me – it isn't going away – and so, unless I was willing to feel down forever, I had to make a change.

I even made new friends, and that was a huge step forwards. A point proven to myself: I am capable. But it didn't come easy, not to somebody like me. I was so nervous to see them at first, not because of them, but because of me.

I guess it was partly the fear of the unknown. I was used to interacting with our family friends and my very few long-term friends. I knew how our relationships worked – they were comfortable. But these friends were different, and I didn't know which way it would go. At first, I worried about every word I said and every message I sent, just in case I accidentally offended them. They had welcomed me into their circle, and I was so happy about it. But my fears ran deep, and I had to work hard every day, to suppress them.

I'd lost friends in the past, for different reasons, some of which I wasn't even sure of. But I'd spent a lot of time blaming myself, regardless of the circumstances. I could be 100% sure it wasn't my fault – maybe it wasn't theirs either, and rationally, I know that's okay. I know it's just part of life to drift apart, for things not to work out, for two people to find they just don't have that common ground anymore. Maybe they have just changed and possibly outgrown each other.

I know that it's all okay, but my mind always managed to convince me otherwise. I was overly self-critical, and it was exhausting. My fault or not, I was tired of feeling that way. I was tired of reliving the past and not moving into the present. Socially, I'd remained in the same place for a long time. I felt like I'd just watched as the world moved on, and people lived their lives.

But that was all about to change.

Layla started it all. She was working with my mum and had found out about me and my health, physical and mental. She said it'd be good for me to chat to her friend Erin, because she was having seizures too, and maybe we could help each other. We each swapped numbers, and Erin and I texted back and forth a lot. Our interests, our family settings, our lives – everything was different – but something bonded us together from the very beginning, and that was seizures.

She knew how it really felt to come back into consciousness, how it feels to be judged so harshly for something you can't control, how it affects everyone around you…she completely understood. I never once imagined that my disorder could be the basis of such a great bond.

I felt really comfortable talking to her about my mental health too, which was something I always tried to keep quiet, because a lot of people misunderstand. Layla and I talked too, of course, and somehow, without meeting either of them face-to-face yet, I trusted them.

It wasn't long before we did meet. I met Layla in her car when she picked me up for the first time. (Her road rage has to be one of the funniest things I've ever heard)! We went to the hospital to visit Erin. She'd had an operation to remove a mass on her brain – that's why she'd been having seizures – and it had gone really well. I couldn't wait to see her. We got on even more in person. In time, we met each other's families, and I met Layla's boyfriend and more of their friends. I soon felt like they were my friends too, and it was pretty much perfect.

They were all just so accepting of me, and protective too. They knew I had this disorder, they knew I had other problems too, but they never treated me any differently for it. They introduced me to new things and involved me in everything, even if I couldn't do it. They didn't pressure me. If we had plans and I couldn't make it, Layla would send pictures and videos. They made me feel like I was part of it anyway, and it made all the difference.

Since her operation, Erin hadn't had many seizures, but a few months later, she had a huge one. I really felt for her. I was having them all the time, and it was horrible, but I knew it must be even worse to finally feel like you've won the battle, only to have it knock you down again.

But that one seizure changed the game. The doctors did some scans, and the worst results came from them. The word people stress about when they look up their symptoms on Google. The word you never want to hear. Erin had cancer.

The tumour was inside her brain, and it was growing. She tried all the treatments, but they didn't work for her. We celebrated her birthday in hospital. We gave her gifts, laughing and joking around as usual, and my mum made chocolate brownies for her – she had wanted them for ages! Layla and Erin had been friends for a really long time, so she was more like family. I'd ask her how everybody was doing, especially Erin's parents. They were pillars of strength, support and unconditional love, and I always admired them.

We would have given her anything, but nobody could give her time. We were at the end.

Our incredible Erin passed away. There were so many broken hearts.

After losing her, I felt like a broken soul. We all did. I'd been through the grieving process before, and I knew it would be overwhelming and beyond difficult. I couldn't imagine how much harder it was for Layla and the others, considering how much Erin had touched my life in a short space of time.

I cried all the time. Silly little arguments with my sisters or my mum, which would usually mean nothing at all, felt like they were tearing me apart. Then, I began to worry about losing Layla. What if Erin was the glue that held us together? What if she was the sole reason Layla and I had developed such a lovely friendship? In my heart, I knew that wasn't true. After all, Layla was the reason I knew Erin. But my mind was controlled by a grip that never seemed to loosen anymore, and it was a grip I knew too well.

I knew it was okay to cry, to miss my friend and to wish we'd had more time. But my faulty mental health wasn't just a side effect of my grief that would eventually disappear. It was a long-time problem that was deeply embedded into me.

Chapter Twenty-One

Ever since I'd finished my first course of therapy, I'd never had suicidal thoughts again. But the vulnerability of depression always seemed to be lurking at the back of my mind. Anxiety, on the other hand, was at the forefront. I was riddled with an intense fear of…well, everything. I'd defy anybody to live with uncontrolled epilepsy and not have some level of anxiousness, but this was off the charts.

Suddenly, the doorbell was making me jump out of my skin, as was the sound of our landline. I couldn't bear to open the door, unless I categorically knew it would be my mum, my nan or my sisters. I remember Mia and I ordering pizza once, and she had to get out of the shower to come downstairs to open the door, wrapped in a towel, because I'd just freeze. I told myself to stop being so ridiculous. I tried reminding myself of how far I'd come, but it never worked.

Between seizures, panic attacks and emotional breakdowns, I was unable to be alone. My nan used to come around to our house to look after me until my mum got home. Then, I barely left my mother's side. It was like I'd reverted back to babyhood. My nan was an angel, but the arrangement started to worry me. I knew she was struggling enough. She had arthritis and was often in chronic pain. I could see it when she moved a certain way. She winced a lot.

I worried she wouldn't be able to move quick enough to get to me when I fell into seizures. I knew if something fatal was to happen – which is always a possibility – that my poor grandmother would never be able to forgive herself. What if I cracked my head open before she reached me, or if one of my limbs got trapped, or if I collapsed whilst walking to the bathroom? That was literally the *only* exercise I was getting, and the only time I was ever really on my own. The more I had to worry about, the more panic attacks I suffered, and they were awful. So then, it fell to Mia.

I never wanted anyone to put their lives on hold for me. My mum did that enough. She'd reduced her hours at work and changed them around twice, as things became worse and worse. I felt pathetic and unworthy. But while my younger sister was still figuring out her life, she was at home anyway, so she took the reins. It was the same kind of scenario. She'd remind me to take my medication, help me to get down the stairs if I was injured or feeling dizzy, and then she'd sit with me until our mum came home. That was how our daily lives worked.

It was hard, because my mum wasn't in a position to devote every spare moment of her time to me – she couldn't. Ellie had gone back into full-time work now, so my mum took care of Lilly. I often looked into my niece's ocean-blue eyes and felt so glad I was around to see her grow and change. She was the love of my life, but I didn't feel like a good auntie. There was nothing I loved more than those moments she cuddled into me, or wanted me to play with her.

But as Lilly got older, she became so active and those cuddly moments became few and far between. I didn't have the energy to run around with her. I spent my time dawdling around in dressing gowns, often alternating between sobbing my heart out and shutting myself away in my bedroom.

That was where most of my panic attacks happened.

My absent seizures were a lot more frequent too. Sometimes, they were called 'vacant episodes' or 'funny turns'. Unlike the seizures I'm used to, I was physically conscious, but I wasn't there – not really. It was only a minute or two before I'd snap back into the world, but I never had a clue where I was, what I was doing, and sometimes who I was with. It scared me into inconsolable panic.

When I eventually reached some kind of inner calmness, I couldn't remember a thing about it – the absence or the hysteria.

I guess that was the whole 'fight or flight' thing. I'd learnt about that in therapy. I figured my mind just disconnected the memory wire, so I didn't have to deal with it.

My mum was the only one who could talk me round. In time, Mia learnt to do that too. I asked them to tell me what happens when one of my panic attacks took place.

It happens quite suddenly, although over time, I had so many that they both became pros at spotting the signs. My heart would speed up by the second and my breathing became fast and shallow, like I couldn't take a deep breath in. I'd stutter sometimes, and I could be very repetitive. The words were all muddled up, like pieces of a puzzle they would have to put together. I'd shake and fidget, and I'd rock forwards and backwards, unable to sit still. Sometimes, I'd cry too.

I also clawed at my hands, like I used to do when I was a little girl, scratching them hard. I'd pull at my fingers too and bend them backwards, over and over and over again. I've even had to be restrained once or twice – they were worried that I'd dislocate my fingers.

Nothing really excited me anymore. My interests had diminished, along with any shred of self-esteem I had left. I was the high achiever who spiralled into failure – the weak link in a strong-hearted family. I felt so scared of life outside of my front door, but inside, the walls were caving in.

I became really good at pretending to be fine around other people, because I found it easier than trying to explain what was really going on. Disturbed sleep, voices in my head, vulnerability, dark thoughts, lack of focus... I was drifting through my days, each bad day rolling into the next.

The world felt very big, and I felt incredibly small. Like before, my existence was just an existence. I didn't want to face whatever was waiting for me. I couldn't.

Hand in hand, depression and anxiety had plagued me all over again. My mum insisted that I needed to go to the doctors and be referred back to therapy, but I insisted that she was being overprotective and I just needed to find a way to relax. But one night, I completely fell apart.

It was intense. I sobbed as I tried to speak, repeating myself, and sometimes, making no sense at all.

I guess it was similar to a panic attack, but I was more aware of it. I said things that hurt her – I tried not to, but once it had started, almost everything came out. I told her I couldn't do this. I couldn't carry on. I'd had enough, and I didn't want to be here anymore.

"If I didn't have my family," I said between sobs, "I'd have killed myself by now."

I didn't mean to say it, at least not to my mother, but that sentence had been on repeat inside my head, especially at night time, when I was on my own, and nobody was there to protect me from myself. My mind was always filled with self-hate, and thoughts of my failures, and how easy it would be for everybody else to live their lives if I wasn't around. Saying the words out loud made it more real and more frightening.

The people I loved were the only reason I was holding on for dear life.

My life was seizures, hospitals, panic attacks and losing people. All that work in therapy last time, coming to terms with the fact I'd tried to take my own life, and now I'd gone back there. I'd gone back to *that* place – the place I vowed I'd never go back to. But my disorder had control of my body, my fractured mental health had control of my mind, and depression was an unforgiving disease. I worried that it really was over. I would never be able to come back from it again, not this time.

I went to see my doctor – another very patient and understanding man – and when I told him how I was feeling, he said he wanted to see me every two weeks. I'm sure that had something to do with my past, because they knew I was vulnerable. We talked about anti-depressants, and I declined, but I was much less resistant. I got my name on the waiting list for therapy, and with the promise of a fortnightly visit, I left the surgery.

In the meantime, I began to seriously consider the medication, especially after my initial telephone consultation with one of the therapists. She reiterated what my doctor had told me, that medication *and* therapy together had more chance of helping to control your emotions, but I still didn't know what to do. I just wanted to get better, but the thought of being on even more medication worried me, especially all of the possible side effects.

I'd always fought against mental health medication. It had been suggested to me multiple times since I'd tried to end it all. To me, it seemed like a short-term fix, whereas I desperately wanted a long-term solution. I talked to my family about it and then talked to my doctor again at our next appointment.

Between us, we decided that I *had* to try.

So, every day, twice a day, I took an anti-depressant. It was to help stabilise my moods and level out my anxiety.

The adjustment period was awful. I was wiped out, which I expected, but I experienced dizziness, lots of sweating to my face and neck (which was horrible and embarrassing!) and a constant feeling of nausea. The tablets also suppressed my appetite. I just wasn't hungry at all. The food could be super healthy, complete junk or in between, but I didn't want any of it. My family even offered me chocolate and ice cream, which I declined, for the first time in my entire existence!

I do not want to take anti-depressants forever. For me, the side effects continue to be awful, and that's really hard to deal with sometimes. When I feel ready to withdraw from them, I'll be straight back to my doctor. But for now, it is what it is. I'm not ready yet, and we know it.

Chapter Twenty-Two

I know, as much as anybody, that it's hard to be on the outside looking in. Mental illnesses aren't so easily understood. But from the inside, it's even harder to explain. If you haven't dealt with depression, I can promise you this: however difficult you're imagining it to be, it's worse. It's like you're keeping so many secrets, from the people you love so much, and you're living in desperate sadness, but you can't see a way out.

You worry that you're stuck there forever, in that dark and dreadful place. But from experience, I can make another promise: you're not.

I soon met my new cognitive behavioural therapist, Emma, and she was great. She helped me to face things that were taunting me, day in and day out. You do begin to feel a sense of relief, but there was nothing easy about it.

My mental health had been so unbalanced for such a long time – up and down – but it was always extreme. You don't really feel it happening (at least I didn't), but somewhere along the line, during my sessions, things began to change within me...

For example, even briefly talking about Erin made me re-evaluate the importance of friendship. Where would I be now, I wondered, if I hadn't pushed through these fears once before? I'd never have known Layla and Erin, I would have never been introduced to new people and new things, or made great memories, or learnt from all of them. It all started quite simply, but now I couldn't imagine not knowing them.

I couldn't justify hiding away from new chances of friendship, but I was riddled with anxiety all over again, head to toe. I felt incapable of getting to know people. I constantly worried about what kind of impression I was making. Just the possibility of judgement and the fear of rejection kept me frozen to the spot.

The thing is, I was scared of losing people, but I also had a fear of finding them.

Emma helped me to set goals when I first began seeing her. We made a lot, but one of my most important ideals was to make new friends, or at least be open to it. So, I had to learn to redefine my social skills: making eye contact, speaking clearly, finding a way to make a nice, honest impression, without all the pressure I put on myself. Having a conversation with somebody didn't mean it *had* to become friendship – it didn't have to become anything at all – I just had to interact. The hardest part, for me, was learning not to overthink it, because that was a tedious habit of mine.

A few sessions had passed; I wasn't 'better' by any means, but I was *doing* better. I had mini interactions with shop assistants and with a member of staff at Lilly's nursery. It doesn't sound like a big deal, but they were massive stepping stones for me. The first few times, I'd shake and my hands would become clammy, I'd stutter and lose my wording. My mum would usually take it from there. I'd try, but if she had to, she'd take over before I crossed over into full-blown panic mode. She had learnt to see it in my eyes.

I think I'd have conquered it sooner if I could go places and do things on my own. Epilepsy is an obstacle, because it prevents me from complete independence, but I tried my best.

Emma told me it would get easier the more I repeated it, the less I avoided it, and I couldn't stop trying – not now that I was proving her right. It really was a little easier each time, although it wasn't always pleasant. People can be abrupt or rude, and that's never nice, but it wasn't the point. The point was trying.

So, one afternoon, I went into a beauty store with my mum. It was the same store we'd been to many times before, and we followed the same routine as always. She would walk around with me, rolling her eyes and sighing a little too loudly, trying to rush me out of there before I spent every penny to my name on 'makeup that you barely even use, Georgina!'

(You know you're in trouble when your parents start full-naming you, even as an adult).

I managed to ask a young woman, around my age, about a product that had just came out. She offered to try it out on me, and of course, I hesitated. I used to love having my makeup done professionally, but it felt like it had been forever.

It's *supposed* to be fun, but what if I said the wrong thing? What if I didn't say anything at all? What if the two of us ended up in a long and awkward silence? What if I have a tonic-clonic seizure in front of all these people? What if I have an absent seizure and forget where I am? Oh my God, it will freak everybody out! Also, this woman will see *my* skin, and I haven't been so great with it lately – I've lost the routine, and I have really bad blemishes. Nothing will cover it up. She'll think I'm disgusting.

Those worries swirled around at the back of my mind all the time, and it was so difficult to dismiss them, but this girl had a really nice nature about her. A lightness that made it easier to just smile and say *"okay."*

Never in a million years would I have predicted how amazingly that one interaction turned out, because after a few more visits, I ended up with *four* new friends. As I was having my makeup applied, another girl had recognised me. I'd met her once about a year before, in the same shop. She had been so kind to me, and my mum called and told the manager to pass on our thanks. I hadn't seen her again since, not that I'd have seen her anyway, considering I hadn't taken my eyes off of the floor for so long.

As I got to know them, I also met the other girls they work with, and they all showed me so much understanding and heartfelt kindness, and we became good friends. We began catching up with each other outside of the store too, of course, and I was even invited to one of their birthday parties.

The party was to take place in a private club they had hired out in the city centre, and I was terrified. I guess it was because of the environment, and all the new people that would be there, but my debilitating nerves were mostly to blame. I really wanted to go. I really wanted to try. I think, if it had been a night out, rather than a party, I couldn't have done it. An actual party just felt safer to me. Knowing the girls wanted me to be there, I made it my absolute mission.

I could take Mia along too, just to feel a little more comfortable. Also, she had given me my rescue medication before, and I figured a nightclub wasn't the best place for another person to try administering it for the first time.

My new friends were all so happy that I had made it, and even an hour later, when the panic began to rise and I felt like I just *had* to go back home, they were so lovely about it. I apologised over and over again, but they said not to be silly. They were really proud of me, and with time, I began to feel just as comfortable with them as I do with my other friends.

They proved to me that friendship has no time frame. They feel close to me and to my heart, closer than some people I've known for my whole life. I've never been alone, but I've known loneliness. I know what it's like, to feel a gap that can only be filled by certain things or certain kinds of people, and they were mine.

I am always content in the knowledge that I've told all my friends everything they need to know. I trust them, and most of the time, I'm not all that nervous anymore. It took me a really long time to stop over-analysing, to stop replaying every interaction over and over again, to stop wondering if they thought I was weird or a complete freak. They all tell me how strong I am, but they don't realise how much they've helped in building me up.

They make me feel like I'm worthy, and I don't think we can ask much more from the people we choose to spend our time with.

Chapter Twenty-Three

During my time in therapy, I began taking walks again, and eventually, I even went swimming!

To me, that was the best thing I'd achieved in a long time. Swimming had been a greatly-loved childhood hobby, but I hadn't been near a pool in over ten years. I'd tried before – I planned it and bought a swimsuit and all those things – but when it came to actually going through with it, I had crumbled. Every single time.

But, sometimes, the way therapists explain things makes you wonder why you ever considered it to be such a huge deal.

We talked through each issue I had, such as being mortified at the thought of other people seeing me in a swimming costume, even though they were complete strangers. But each problem had a solution, or at least, an answer – a reasonable answer that made me feel like I could *choose* to be brave here.

I *could* go swimming, because I had every right to. I *could* go swimming, despite the obstacles I would undoubtedly face, just because I wanted to. It wasn't about exercise or becoming fitter – that would be an extra perk – it was about achieving a goal, another 'ideal' of mine.

The first step was asking my mum if she'd be willing to come along too, to make me feel safer. The second step was visiting the centre, just to visit and get a feel for the place, not to swim. I talked to one of the staff members, and she was lovely when we were telling her about my disorder (if you have epilepsy, you *have* to tell the lifeguards)!

The next step was actually swimming. I was so nervous, but we took Lilly along too, and I just played with her in the baby pool. Focusing on her safety meant that I couldn't spend as much time focusing on my worries. The second time, I did the same thing. The third time, I swam one length in the main pool and then played with Lilly again.

What I came to realise was that nobody cared. Nobody was looking at me in a swimming costume. Nobody noticed that I'd only managed to swim one single length. Nobody knew that I was breathless afterwards. Nobody knew that this had been a huge step forwards. I liked that; the indifference. Those other people were there for themselves, not to make fun of anybody else.

In time, swimming became easier. Even when my therapy sessions had finished, I kept up with it whenever I could. Walking and swimming became my first ventures back into exercise, which felt good to acknowledge, especially because my food intake seemed to be increasing every day.

It began to worry me. I wasn't hungry, but sometimes, I just couldn't stop. Food had been an issue for longer than I'd like to admit, but it was something I'd always swept under the rug.

As a kid, I had a big appetite and the sweetest tooth known to mankind. I loved going out for dinner. I liked the atmosphere of our favourite restaurants and just being out with my family, enjoying ourselves.

Despite the fact that my mum and nan always seemed to be dieting, I wasn't a child who particularly cared about my calorie intake. I was so active, and burning enough calories to eat whatever I wanted.

I remember, after I stopped dancing, my mum would say to me, "I don't want to upset you, but you're beginning to gain weight. Maybe you should think about eating a little healthier." I hadn't put the two together before: when I wasn't exercising so much, I'd have to tweak my eating habits.

I gained weight during the awkward puberty stage, when I was trapped in a circle of growing pains, acne and menstruation. From there, I became more aware of the food I was taking in, but I still didn't change anything.

I'd say it was during my first year of college, that I really began turning to food for comfort. I was *always* stressed – the jump from GCSE studies to A Level studies was much tougher than I'd imagined. The workload was intense, as was the pressure of being accepted into university.

Plus, there was the added strain of trying to make a good impression on people. It was the first time in my entire life that people actually looked at my clothes: how you dressed, what clothes you wore and how good you looked was suddenly important. Each year would begin in shirts, trousers or skirts, and sensible shoes, but would gradually morph into skinny jeans, dresses and converse. Some girls never wore the same outfit twice, but I wasn't one of them. I never thought I'd miss wearing my school uniform.

What happened very quickly, during my studies, was that I began eating for quickness and convenience. In spite of my big appetite, I was a fussy eater and didn't really like the foods I was capable of making for myself. So, I'd buy biscuits and sweets on my way home from college and eat them all in private, before I started my revision.

I was nervous of judgement, even from my own family, so I'd hide the wrappers anywhere I could and pretend I hadn't eaten at all. It just felt like less of a lie than pretending I'd eaten something healthy. If I found snacks lying around the house, I'd have inhaled them before I even had the chance to think about it. So many times, I'd end up rushing to the shop before anybody else came home, replacing whatever it was.

I think that was a comforting solution, because I could pretend it hadn't happened.

When I got a job in a local café, I ate things I'd never eaten before. Even the simplest foods were different – toast, for example. At home, bread was usually from a small or medium loaf, and we always had it with margarine, usually a low-fat version. But at work, we'd have thick white bread, toasted perfectly, with real butter. The other members of staff couldn't believe I'd never had real butter before! Another staple 'work food' was chips, usually leftover from frying too many throughout the day. Snacks would be cookies. Drinks would be bottles of regular coke, syrup-based slushes in summer, hot chocolates in winter.

I used some of my wages for nights out with my sister and my friends, on which I'd drink vodka and coke, wine or sugary alcopops. More often than not, these nights ended in pizza, chippy chips or McDonalds, and I tried not to think about it.

But one day, it just hit me: I was fat.

It's funny how long you can avoid a mirror when you really don't want to see what you've become.

After this harsh realisation, I needed quick and effective weight loss, not a long-term, healthy, balanced diet. That would take way too long. So, instead, I turned to barely eating and taking pills that claimed to speed the process along. Those pills were kept a secret. I remember I used to hide the box, and take out the pills as I needed them. I kept the little pink tablets in my bag, or zipped into the pockets of my outfits.

I began counting every calorie, logging it all in a journal, berating myself whenever I gave in. I'd gorge on chocolate, biscuits and sweets until I felt too sick to carry on. Even then, I'd try to push myself even further. Once or twice, I was leant over the toilet, trying to shove my fingers down my throat far enough to throw it all back up.

But vomiting was one of my worst fears. Maybe 'fear' isn't the right word, but the thought of vomiting – when it happens to me or to anybody else – I just can't bear it. So, subconsciously at least, I knew my mind wouldn't allow my fingers to force out the junk I'd succumbed to. After a few separate attempts, I didn't try it again.

I'd starve until I couldn't anymore, then I'd binge, but I could never get rid of it.

I've never considered myself to have an eating problem. In my mind, an eating problem was when a person was drastically underweight, and that certainly didn't apply to me. I was just weak and fat. In time, I threw the pills away, the secrets along with them, and I just ate whatever I wanted, dismissing any kind of concern from the people around me. I figured there was no point in trying to lose weight by starving myself, because I couldn't keep it up long enough to see a difference. I always gave in, but of course, it was never fresh fruit or salad that I turned to.

I spent a while pretending not to care. There were plenty of excuses, especially after I was diagnosed, and dieting was kicked off my endless list of things to worry about.

For me, stress had *always* led to food. Emotions – good and bad – led to food. I used food as a coping mechanism, and I guess that's when it really became a prevalent issue. Whether I was starving, bingeing, avoiding mirrors or pretending I didn't care, I was still left with the shame.

It is kind of odd: emotionally, I've probably cared too much, but physically, I clearly hadn't cared enough to change it. Maybe, I was scared of what life would become when I actually did feel content in my own skin. Maybe, I was scared of doing all that hard work, to then feel exactly the same as I did before.

My weight, amongst other things, had contributed to my diminished self-confidence, and it was definitely one of the reasons I began to hate myself.

I had been judged for it in the past, and it always hurt more than it should have.

A drunk guy called me a fat b**** once, whilst I was standing outside a bar. It had been a celebration for one of Ellie's friends, and I'd decided to go out with my sister, just for an hour. I was getting some fresh, cool air while I waited for her to say goodbye. I didn't know this man, and he didn't know the damage he was causing.

But he was right, and I unfortunately did care what people thought of me.

The idea of being judged by strangers and even people I knew was a constant worry. If somebody looked at me, it was because I was fat. If I ran into someone I hadn't seen in a while, I knew they'd be talking about me when they walked away.

It seems selfish now, that I truly believed other people were spending their time talking and thinking about me. They had their own lives, their own families, their own problems.

They probably didn't care that I'd put on some weight – it wasn't their business – and if they did talk about it, I guess that says more about them than it does about me.

I knew exactly how to lose weight – eat less, but eat well, and move more – but a vital component is motivation, and mine was non-existent. I had self-medicated my emotions with food for a long time, and the number on the scales continued to rise.

Petrified of diabetes, heart disease and living my entire life in hatred of myself, I found the number of a local Slimming World consultant. She was understanding when I told her about my unique set of circumstances, and that evening, my mum and I joined her group.

I'd always thought of Slimming World as a mothers' group. I know that's pretty judgmental of me, but I did. I didn't think of it as the place where girls in the mid-twenties, just like me, would choose to spend one of their evenings. I was really surprised at the age range, from teenagers to probably late-sixties in my particular group, all at various weights and different stages in their journeys.

Everyone just seemed nice, too. Similar to the other swimmers at the pool, they didn't look at me and think 'she's huge!' or at least, I didn't feel that way.

I listened intently and learnt the plan. Just one week later, I'd lost 6 ½ pounds. I definitely became a little smug after that, and I let myself go a bit more the following week. But it was still a lot less than what I was eating before, and so, I lost another 3 pounds.

In the weigh-in world, a loss is a loss – a great achievement – but losing 3 pounds after losing 6 ½ felt like failure, a familiar taste to me.

I acted happy, especially because the group was all about support and helping each other; some women had maintained their weight, or even gained, so I wasn't going to sit there and complain about losing.

Slimming World is pretty clever. It's like reverse psychology, especially to the serial-dieter.

The consultants never tell you to count calories or ban 'bad' foods, or to stop going out for dinner. Instead, they give you a massive list of all the foods you can eat to your heart's content every single day. On top of that, you can still have your favourite foods, just in moderation. For me, it was always pizza or chocolate, but it was surprisingly easy to go from eating share-size chocolate bars to the individual size. You are encouraged to make healthier choices in restaurants, but you can go anywhere. You can still live your life the way you want to. When it comes to food, the plan just makes you think a little more.

My first major setback happened on my fourth week. It was the run-up to my period and my body had decided to develop some kind of superhuman chocolate tolerance, and I just couldn't resist. It wasn't an excuse – I knew what I was doing – but I also knew I'd gained weight.

I knew I'd failed, and so, for the rest of the week, I ate *everything* in sight. Looking back, it doesn't make much sense. Surely, knowing I'd fallen off the wagon a little bit, I'd have tried extra hard to get back on track? But that wasn't the case.

I gained 3 pounds that week, and it was awful. But, it forced me to learn an important lesson: just because I mess up, doesn't mean I have to *keep* messing up. I don't have to feel like a complete failure. In fact, I could even choose to be proud of myself for trying to turn it around.

I took that as a life lesson, not just a weight loss inspiration. So now, during an obstacle, I try to remember that I always have that choice. I don't *have* to let a single setback become anything more than what it is.

You learn, and then you move on.

Part Four
Now

Chapter Twenty-Four

For as long as I can remember, I have loved to write. I found joy in creativity, and as I grew up, I found solace in writing too. I was always very passionate – don't get me wrong – but I never really thought about writing as a career.

Originally, I wanted to teach.

I'm good with kids, and that was the only thing I was sure of. All the experience I'd had helped me to become both confident and comfortable in that kind of role, and I knew I could happily work with children for the rest of my life.

I knew it would be challenging at times – it's certainly not an easy job – but I liked to believe I could be great at it someday. My cousin was my biggest inspiration for teaching. You can tell instantly that she is an amazing teacher. Being close to her also means I've seen the stress first hand: the workload, late nights, school holidays filled with paperwork and pressure for the new term and/or year ahead. But none of that changed my mind – I'm pretty sure all careers have their downsides, no matter how incredible they might be.

When I was in high school, I planned to go to college. When I was in college, I planned to go to university. Each time I moved on, I had a plan for what came next. Making plans became much more difficult post-diagnosis, but still, I decided that I'd like to study for my teaching qualification after I'd spent time on those two voluntary schemes. As you'll know by now, that didn't exactly go to plan...

I finally had to accept that it wasn't going to happen, and I was devastated.

"Don't be silly!"

"It's not your fault."

"You don't have to fret about your career yet anyway!"

The people around me told me those things over and over again, but their words of well-intentioned kindness went in one ear and out of the other. Yet again, I'd failed.

But in therapy, Emma and I never focused on anything I can't do (I mean 'can't do' in the medical sense only, of course, because she, like many others, believed I could do anything I set my mind to).

We slowly began to work on my interests – rediscovering all the things I used to love, the things that had been lost along the way. So much time had passed and I hadn't done anything with it. Writing, I realised, was my main ideal. Writing had always been special to me, for as long as I could remember, but I'd lost sight of it in my battle. I'd lost sight of almost everything.

But writing soon became an outlet for my inner turmoil. One night, an argument took place between Mia and I. I couldn't even tell you what it was about, something futile and forgettable, but it ended in my frustration and panic, and then I dissolved into floods of tears, as usual. You see, in those moments, nothing was a 'silly little argument' to me.

I told my mum I needed ten minutes to myself, and I went to my bedroom, listening to the shallow breaths I was taking. In that time, I wrote.

I wrote everything down – what had happened, the things that were said, how I responded, how others responded, how I felt before, during and after. Emma had set it as a task for the week ahead: to record my reactions to any situations I found stressful. When my mum came in to check on me, I realised I actually did feel better. I couldn't pinpoint it, but somewhere along the line, writing had helped. Writing had been cathartic. My shoulders had loosened significantly, my heart wasn't beating quite as fast, and my head wasn't pounding quite as hard.

From there, I began to write again, just for myself. I hadn't made it out the other side just yet, but writing was a huge piece of my 'getting better' puzzle. Sometimes, it wasn't as simple as opening a notebook, or loading up a laptop and going for it. Sometimes, I just couldn't. I'd be having such a bad day that it was too overwhelming, or I'd be having a good day and wouldn't want to bring myself down by accidentally reading something I'd written before.

In time, writing became what it used to be to me. When I starting using my imagination again, creating stories about the characters and worlds I'd dreamt up, that's when I truly rediscovered my love of writing, and it was transcendent.

Of course, with writing, I began reading again too. I picked short, easy reads to begin with. I only read for five minutes at the beginning, but it wasn't long before I was reading at least one book every week.

Being the child who had annoyed my mum and grandparents with requests for second, third and fourth bedtime stories, it felt great to unashamedly be a bookworm again. I'm learning again: about the book, the author, the world they have brought to life, and in the process, I nearly always learn something about myself.

That's part of the magic.

I started to think about it more and more: maybe, *just maybe,* writing was what I was supposed to do all along.

When my mind travels back to the time of my diagnosis, and through many situations since then, I would have loved to read something like this: just an open, honest account of life, from someone who had experienced real suffering, but had survived it all, with help and kindness and love.

I've always had a desire to help other people – that was one of the main reasons I wanted to teach – and maybe writing can finally be my chance to do that.

Epilogue

In my daily life, I try to keep in mind that everybody is fighting a battle – big or small, forever and for now – it doesn't matter. When I talk to my family, catch up with a friend, run into someone I used to know, or even if we get chatting to a stranger, I try to listen as hard as I can. I've heard all kinds, from daily trials and tribulations to completely heart-breaking situations. But I've also heard about their baby being born healthy, or getting their dream job, or the supermarket finally having their favourite cakes back in stock! We just never know what another person is facing, and regardless of how their lives are going, you *could* be making their day.

When people vent to me, they'll often reach a certain point and stop suddenly. "I can't believe I'm complaining about this to *you*," they'll say, "you deal with so much every day and this is just something so trivial and stupid!" Then, I shake my head and smile.

"Don't be silly!" is my response, and I encourage them to carry on. Firstly, I don't expect, nor do I *want* the rest of the world to tiptoe around me and my disorder. Secondly, I really do care, so I want to know what's going on, good or bad. Lastly, just knowing other people have problems, even without a brain disorder, reminds me that I'm probably doing okay after all.

I'm far from perfect, I can't always think positive, and I definitely get fed up sometimes. I don't feel sorry for myself, but some days are harder than others, and on those days, I wonder *why*. Why do I have epilepsy? Why were there never any signs? Was it mothers' intuition all those years ago, when my mum feared something bad happening to me, or was that just a coincidence, a typical case of a worrisome mind? What is the meaning of it all?

But I don't have the answers, and that's okay too. It has to be.

I tell people I'm epileptic, because I have to. But I tell them for *their* sake as well as my own, maybe even more – for their readiness, to lessen that element of shock when a seizure takes hold, as it inevitably will, because the people around me deserve the preparation that I didn't get. I have this disorder and it is a big part of me, but it's not everything I am. I don't feel that way anymore.

My family and my friends – 'my lovelies' as I call them – accepted me for who I am: epileptic, depressed, chronically anxious, periodically dropping to the floor, forgetting things, cancelling plans, bouts of inner frustration surfacing as accidental snappiness… and they showed me, time and time again, that those are probably the last things they see in me.

They know and they care, but I just get to be me. I don't have to pretend. I don't have to play the role of somebody else, because they made me believe that who I am *is* good enough.

I'm just a young woman who still stresses about a spot, whose entire mood can completely change depending on the weather, who can recite my favourite episode of Scandal word for word, and gets annoyed when nobody else wants dessert at a restaurant. (I mean, aren't desserts the *reason* we decided to go out for dinner?!)

I'm a writer, a bookworm, an ex-dancer with a lot of stories from my 'local showbiz' days. I'm a daughter, a granddaughter, a sister, a niece, a cousin, a friend and an auntie, because I am all of those things, and more. I'm not a genius or a celebrity, and I haven't changed the world. But, what I do have is a kind heart, a creative mind and a voice that I am finally ready to use.

I know my health is unpredictable, and physically, I really don't have control. But what I *can* do is try to manage stress, stick to a basic routine, try to eat well, get enough sleep and exercise when I can. My mental health is vast and has made me vulnerable several times. I know it's something I will have to revisit time and time again. But for now, at least, I'm doing well.

From the moment my first seizure struck, our lives were never going to be the same. I didn't realise how much it would affect *me*, not to mention the people I love, their relationships with me and even their relationships with each other.

Life has been, and continues to be, a difficult, crazy, emotional journey. There were times when I never thought I'd make it to here, and *here* is the point of acceptance. I'm okay with being epileptic, I'm okay with letting go of the life I'd once planned, I'm okay with the fact that I've struggled with my mental health, and more importantly, I'm thrilled I had help with it. Admitting you need help is nothing to be ashamed of anymore – in fact, I think it's pretty brave. Therapy, for example, could be the key to making you better. After all, it saved my life.

Despite all the chaos inside my brain, that voice, once so deafening, is finally quiet. There are no certainties, but I like to think I'll be just fine. I want to keep writing forever, and I want to help others as much as I can. I owe that to everybody I love, and to myself. So, I hope we can meet again…